D1462161

THE CONTEMPORARY TWELVE

THE CONTEMPORARY TWELVE

The Power of Character in Today's World

WALTER L. UNDERWOOD

ABINGDON PRESS
NASHVILLE

THE CONTEMPORARY TWELVE
THE POWER OF CHARACTER IN TODAY'S WORLD

Scripture quotations unless otherwise noted are from the Revised Standard Version of the Bible, copyrighted 1946, 1952, 1971, © 1973, by the Division of Christian Education of the National Council of the Churches of Christ in the U.S.A., and used by permission. Those noted KJV are from the King James Version.

The quotation by John J. Conger on page 41 is used by permission of *U.S. News & World Report.*

The lines by Rainer Maria Rilke on page 53 are from Rainer Maria Rilke, *Poems* 1906-1926. Copyright © 1957 by New Directions Publishing Corporation. All rights reserved. Reprinted by permission of New Directions.

The quotation on page 83 is from "Heresy Indeed" by Sara Henderson Hay and is reprinted by permission of the author.

Library of Congress Cataloging in Publication Data

Underwood, Walter L. (Walter Lee), 1925-
The contemporary Twelve.
1. Apostles—Sermons. 2. Methodist Church—Sermons.
3. Sermons, American. I. Title.
BS2440.U53 1984 226'.0922 84-6322

ISBN 0-687-09520-4

MANUFACTURED BY THE PARTHENON PRESS AT
NASHVILLE, TENNESSEE, UNITED STATES OF AMERICA

For Billye

Preface

You and I are the sum total of the past. As heirs of countless generations, we reflect the endowments of our predecessors. Sometimes their legacies are beneficial to us in our lives today, at other times detrimental. Whatever the case, we can recognize ourselves in those who have lived before us. Thus, to contemporize the past offers instruction for the present. I would like to suggest that some part of each of us can be seen in the lives of the Twelve whom Jesus chose as his disciples.

There is very little historical material about the disciples recorded in the Gospels, therefore I have employed a technique of hypothesizing on the basis of the recorded facts to create a character impression of each disciple. I have deliberately tried to image each of them in terms of our contemporary society so that their lives may become relevant and instructional for our character and faith. It has also been my intention to enable the reader to understand Jesus with clearer insight by attempting to penetrate the nature and personality of those who were his first followers.

Hopefully, the reader will see himself or herself in these "mirrors of faith" and find both insight and inspiration for daily living.

Acknowledgments

There are many to whom I would wish to express gratitude: special debt of gratitude to KPRC, Channel 2 and Jack Harris; to the congregations I have served who have challenged my skills to the utmost and made preaching a fearful and joyful adventure; to Joanne Mueller who generously and graciously volunteered to type the original sermons; to Mickie Wright, my loyal and competent secretary, whose skills far surpass clerical mechanics; and to Gail Cooke for her invaluable contributions to this book. Nothing in my ministry would have been possible without my family; especially my wife, Billye, who possesses the incomparable gift of knowing when to criticize and when to praise, thereby keeping me both humble and hopeful.

Walter L. Underwood
St. Luke's United Methodist Church
Houston, Texas 1984

Contents

THE CONTEMPORARY TWELVE

On Playing Second Fiddle

ANDREW

CHAPTER

[1]

The longest-running musical in Broadway history is a production without a star. In its initial planning stages, a reluctant backer protested that nothing should open without a headliner. Not only did *A Chorus Line* open, but it went on to break box office records. Many of us would have sided with the objecting backer because ours is a "star-oriented" culture. Yet most of us are not stars.

Evidently the disciple Andrew was not a star either. He appears only three times in the Gospels: first, when he brought his brother to Jesus; next, when he found the little boy with the five barley loaves and a couple of fish which made possible Jesus' miracle of feeding the five thousand; finally, when the inquiring Greeks came to Philip and said, "We wish to see Jesus." Philip referred their request to Andrew, and Andrew made it possible for them to see Jesus.

In Christian history Andrew is primarily known as Simon Peter's brother. Today he lives under the shadow of the more famous Peter. During his years of discipleship Andrew was not included in Jesus' inner circle of disciples. Jesus did not take Andrew with him when he healed Jairus' daughter, when he went up the Mount of Transfiguration, or when he met his temptation in Gethsemane. Instead, he took Peter, James, and John.

In a similar situation we would probably consider ourselves slighted. "After all," Andrew could have said, "I was one of the first two disciples. I brought Simon Peter to Jesus. Why am I not included in his inner circle?" Wouldn't he have been justified in feeling resentful? Yet, from all we can gather he was content to play second fiddle. He was happy just to be a humble part of the Twelve. Precedence, place, and honor seem to have meant nothing to Andrew. All that mattered was that he was a follower of Jesus and that he could play his part well, however small it might be.

Andrew was from Bethsaida on the Sea of Galilee. With his brother, he owned a house at Capernaum. He was a disciple of John the Baptist, and it was that relationship that directed him to Jesus Christ. He became convinced that Christ was the Messiah and decided to follow him. His conversion experience was so intense that he found his brother and brought him to Jesus also.

Later, Andrew was one of the first two disciples to be chosen.

It is generally accepted that Andrew suffered martyrdom in Achaia by crucifixion on a cross shaped like an X. What we now call the St. Andrew's cross is a cross in the form of an X. There is also a tradition that a ship bearing two relics of his body was wrecked in a bay of Scotland, afterward called St. Andrew's Bay. The sailors who escaped from the shipwreck are said to have gone to the mainland and introduced the gospel of Jesus Christ to the Scottish people. Andrew, therefore, became the patron saint of Scotland.

Someone has said that Andrew is the special guardian of all who gladly and loyally take second place. At this point we can learn a great deal from him because most of us have to play second fiddle. We should accept our roles both graciously and gratefully. In musical compositions second violin is equally important to first violin. A musical score is composed for all of the instruments in an orchestra. The harmony would be incomplete and the effect of the composition diminished without a second violin.

This is also true in life. In the late fifteenth century, Albrecht Dürer and his friend Franz Knigstein were studying to be artists. They were almost destitute. Their art studies suffered because they had to spend so much time working, trying to eke out a living. By drawing lots they decided that Albrecht would study art full time while Franz would spend all of his time working to support the two of them. When Albrecht had completed his studies and was successful they were to reverse places; Albrecht would work while Franz studied art. Albrecht finished his course, and eventually his work was acclaimed. He then returned to change places with his friend. But when he arrived, he discovered what a great sacrifice Franz had made for him. Franz had worked at such arduous manual labor that his fingers and his sensitive hands had become permanently crippled. It was not possible for him ever to be an artist, but there was no bitterness in his heart. His happiness was in the joy that he had made Albrecht's successful career as an artist possible.

One day Albrecht saw Franz kneeling, his rough and gnarled hands clasped in silent prayer. Albrecht began to sketch those rough hands. Out of that preliminary drawing came what is perhaps Albrecht's most famous painting, simply but movingly entitled *Praying Hands.* Five hundred years later, we salute Franz Knigstein, who played second fiddle so magnificently that he made possible the remarkable work of Albrecht Dürer.

Without Franz Knigstein, Albrecht Dürer might never have been an artist. Without Andrew, Jesus' ministry might not have been possible. In the kingdom and in life, those who play secondary parts are equal in importance to those who play what seem to be more prominent roles. Sometimes a special awareness is needed to recognize this fact. Consider the Bible. The one-talent man in Jesus' parable was just as important as the five-talent man. The one-talent man did not realize his importance; yet had he made use of his talent he would have received the same reward as the five-talent man.

Those who play secondary parts and those who play primary parts should be recognized as of equal importance because it takes the same amount of skill, competence, and commitment to play either role. We can look at a music score and see that the second violin part is not easier to play than the first. It is not less demanding. The fact that it is the second part does not mean it is second-rate. No second-rate violinist would ever be hired by a symphony orchestra to play second violin. Sometimes the second violinist has a solo passage or a score that is more difficult to play than that of the first violin. It is unfortunate that "second" sometimes carries the connotation of less than the best, because playing second violin demands just as much dedication and ability as playing first violin.

According to a recent newspaper article, Tom

Kite, the P.G.A. golfer, won $300,000 in prize money in an eight-month period. Although he is one of the top money winners in golf, he won only one tournament in that length of time. His winnings during this period came primarily from being second instead of first. The fact that his skill, competence, and commitment are equal to the first place winner's is corroborated by his income.

Andrew had the skill, the commitment, and the competence that enabled him to win Simon Peter. Perhaps no one else could have done that. It was he who found the child with the basket lunch; he enabled the Greeks to see Jesus. In the kingdom and in life, people who play small parts but who play them well have enormous capacities for excellence and success.

It is also true that the person who plays second violin may sometimes be more than equal as a person to the one who plays first violin. A famous symphony conductor was once asked which orchestral instrument he considered to be the most difficult to play. Without hesitation the conductor replied: "Second violin. I can get all the first violinists I need, but to find a competent and skilled second violinist who plays with enthusiasm, that's the problem."

It often takes more of a person to be second in life than first. Andrew may have been superior spiritually to Simon Peter. It seems Andrew had the greater loyalty, a clearer self-awareness, and a healthier self-esteem. There are times when it takes more of a man, more of a woman, more of a person, to play second fiddle than to be first.

There is a man I know who will not serve on a committee unless he chairs it. He will not participate in any community project unless he is in control of it. He has what psychologists call the star complex. This man's difficulty is reminiscent of what the valet of one of the kaisers said: "My master was a very vain man. If he went to a baptism, he wanted to be the baby. If he went to a wedding, he wanted to be the bride. And, if he went to a funeral, he wanted to be the corpse."

Not too long ago one of the NFL quarterbacks issued an ultimatum to the owner of his team: "I want to be traded to a team where I am first string. I'm not going to play second string. I'll quit before I do that!" A Yankee pitcher made the same ultimatum to George Steinbrenner, and he was promptly traded. These are examples of people who won't play unless they play "first chair."

On the other hand, there are other people who shun the spotlight. A mother, sending her freshman daughter off to college, wrote to the university president saying: "I am sending my daughter to your school, but I'm very worried about her. She's shy, bashful, and introverted. She doesn't like to be out front. She's really not a leader, but she is a wonderful follower. Please look after her." By return mail, the mother received a letter from the president reading: "Dear Madam, I am looking forward with high anticipation to meeting your daughter. With 1,789 leaders, I can hardly wait to have one follower in our student body."

That university president was aware that it frequently takes more of a person to play second fiddle. There have been persons in the congregations I have served who weren't the stars, who were more or less invisible, but who possessed a spiritual depth, a spiritual insight, a spiritual understanding far beyond what many of us have.

Furthermore, it is true that without the second fiddle players God's will and work will not be done. Had it not been for Andrew, Peter might never have been converted to the Christian faith. Had it not been for Andrew, five thousand people might have gone hungry. Had it not been for Andrew, the inquiring Greeks might never have seen Jesus. Had it not been for Andrew, Jesus' ministry might not have been accomplished.

God accomplishes his will and his work in the world through us. Without God, we can't. Without us, God won't.

I mentioned this idea once before when I was preaching. After the sermon, a lady came down the aisle and I could see that she was a little angry. "Do you mean that God can't do it without us?" she asked. "No," I replied, "that is not what I said. I said, 'God won't do it without us.' He could, but he won't." I further explained to her that God has chosen to do his will and work in the world with us as his instruments. We are his feet; we are his voice; we are his witness. We are his instruments, and the music of the kingdom needs all Christians to sound their notes.

A good friend of mine is now retired after being a prominent and effective minister for many years. When he was a little boy living in a small town, his mother sent him to Sunday school one Sunday. On the way he stopped by a drugstore to have a soft drink. While there, he decided he wouldn't go to Sunday school. The boys in his class assembled, and the teacher looked around and asked, "Where's Roy?" One of the boys ventured, "I bet he's down at the drugstore." The teacher said, "You wait right here. I'm going after Roy." He went into town, found Roy in the drugstore, and brought him to Sunday school. Later, as a grown man, Roy Williams would say: "I owe my call to the ministry to a teacher who cared about me, who loved me enough to leave his Sunday school class to go in search of me, and bring me to class. Had it not been for that teacher, I would never have gone into the ministry."

We don't even know the teacher's name. It's not written down anywhere; no one knows who he was, but God used an obscure, unknown Sunday school teacher as an Andrew, to influence the life of a boy who was called to the ministry and who later blessed and touched the lives of thousands of people. One man was happy to play his part, however small, and play it well.

Do you do your part in the kingdom and in the church? Do you give your gifts? Do you make your contributions? Or do you say, they don't need me; what I have to give isn't important; I can't make any difference?

Jesus knew full well what he was doing when he chose Andrew to be a disciple. He must have selected him because he needed him, because he was necessary. Jesus chose him as an example, an inspiration. His ministry might not have been fulfilled without Andrew.

And Jesus has chosen all of us because we are needed and we are necessary. One thing is for certain: God's kingdom will not come and God's will will not be done on earth as in heaven unless all of us do our part.

Scripture: John 1:40-44; Mark 13:3-4; John 12:20-22; John 6:8; Acts 1:13

Look Before You Leap
PHILIP

CHAPTER

[2]

We human beings have a tendency to make one of two errors in life: we either decide too quickly, without proper consideration of the evidence, or we consider the evidence in such detail that we never decide. We either leap without looking or look so long that we never leap.

Philip is the least colorful of all the disciples; he is dull, unimaginative, hesitant, vacillating, phlegmatic, and apathetic. That's why he is my favorite disciple—he is just like you and me. We can start even with Philip because he is as totally human as we are. It is a mistake to believe that the disciples were unique, unparalleled, or saintly. They were ordinary, common people, and it is for this reason that they can instruct us. We can learn a great deal from them, especially from Philip. The lesson he provides might be considered his motto: Look before you leap.

Philip was one of five of the disciples who were

from Bethsaida. His name was Greek, meaning "lover of horses." We don't know anything about his life prior to this time as a disciple of Jesus. He is described only in John's Gospel, which is a strange phenomenon, as if perhaps John were rescuing him from oblivion. He appears five times in the Gospel of John: first, when Jesus said to him, "Follow me"; second, when he witnessed to Nathaniel: "We have found the Messiah that Moses and the prophets predicted"; third, when we see him in the story of the feeding of the five thousand; fourth, when the Greeks came inquiring if they could see Jesus; and, finally, in the fourteenth chapter of John, when Philip said to Jesus, "Master, show us the Father."

Philip was true to his motto when he displayed caution in the feeding of the five thousand. Jesus called him and asked, "What are we going to do about feeding all those people?" The scripture says that Jesus was testing him; therefore Philip should have answered, "Lord, I believe." Instead, he replied, "Master, we've got a problem. It would take two hundred denarii to give these people just a little bite of bread." That amount of money was equivalent to two hundred days' wages for a Hebrew worker; that was not small change. Philip said, "We had better take a look at this. Let's talk about it; let's think about it." In our vernacular he may have said to Jesus, "It might be a good idea for us to appoint a committee to investigate the situation. They can compile their findings and report back to us."

We shouldn't be too critical of Philip's reticence, because actually exercising caution is good. We all should be prudent to a degree. We should look before we leap. It is important to gather the facts and learn from others. We should pray for guidance. We shouldn't rush into a marriage. We shouldn't be too hasty to get another job. We shouldn't even rush into making a decision for Christ. It is both wise and beneficial for us to look before we leap.

Most of us are naturally circumspect because we are uncomfortable with change. We are threatened by the new; we much prefer what is already known. In fact, the older we grow, the more we lean toward the familiar. My own house and my own bed are more desirable to me than any fine hotel. I know where the refrigerator is at home, and where the night light is. I know where the bathroom is and the stairway. Since we don't like change, we often look a long time before we leap, which is oftentimes advantageous.

However, it must also be said that we shouldn't look so long that we never leap. Evidently Philip could never quite make the leap, even though he was a disciple of Jesus. When the inquiring Greeks wanted to see Jesus, as we know, they approached

Philip. Philip probably thought, "I've never had a request like this before. I don't know what to do about it." He was afraid, hesitant, reluctant. Finally, he just couldn't make the decision and so he went to Andrew, whereupon Andrew ushered the Greeks into the presence of Jesus.

Seemingly Philip's problem was that he had an irresolute mind. He was hesitant; he was slow to act. That is also our problem. Most of us do not have closed minds, we have irresolute minds. We want to keep looking and looking, but never leaping. We can't decide to make the decision. This is a common human failing.

General George B. McClellan was Abraham Lincoln's commander of the Union forces. Lincoln kept urging him to go into action, to get his army moving, to start the battle. But McClellan kept waiting and waiting. At last, Lincoln wrote him a letter reading, "My dear McClellan, if you don't want to use the army, I'd like to borrow it for a while. Yours respectfully, A. Lincoln." It's very easy to look and look and never leap. There is something very intriguing about just looking.

A good many years ago a couple I did not know came to see me. They were an older couple and they said they wanted to get married. I asked them, "How long have you been dating?" They replied, "Thirty-seven years." In retrospect, maybe I should have refused to perform their marriage ceremony. Any couple who can't make up their minds in thirty-seven years has no right to be married. Yet, this is our problem; we look and look and we never leap.

This same hesitancy is evident in our response to the problem of morality in our society. We are slow to reject the unacceptable behavior that is prevalent in our culture. We've appointed committees, commissions, and task forces to deal with these problems, but mostly to no avail. The truth is, we possess the knowledge of what to do, but we lack the will to do it. We could change the nation and our cities tomorrow, but we're still looking and talking.

We could also stop the killing, the bombing, and the destruction of people in war. We could beat our swords into plowshares if we wanted to. It's the will, not the way, that causes us our problems. There is little difference between the wars fought five thousand years ago and the wars we fight today except for the military hardware. Nations are fighting one another for exactly the same reasons, or for lack of the same reasons.

The automobile industry made cars that got only ten miles to the gallon. Engineers could have done something about that a long time ago, but nothing was done until our energy supplies were threatened by the Arab embargo. Now we have automobiles that get fifty miles per gallon. There is a new kind of automobile transmission on the drawing board that will power a subcompact car with only a ten horsepower engine. You see, it is the will that counts.

In Meredith Willson's *Music Man*, the professor tried to get Marion the librarian to go out with him. He asked her to meet him at the footbridge across the stream running through the park. She wanted to, but she refused. She said, "Please, some other time. Maybe tomorrow." The professor persisted, yet she continued to put off their meeting. Finally, in exasperation, he said, "Pile up enough tomorrows and you'll find that you've collected nothing but a lot of empty yesterdays." That is what we are doing in regard to the ethical and moral necessities of society. We're collecting a lot of empty yesterdays because we do not have the will to take the leap to make appropriate decisions.

Our caution is also manifested in our individual personal salvation. There are people who are procrastinating, saying: "I need to study a little more. I don't know enough about the Bible. Let me attend this class, and then I'll become a Christian." We are adept at postponing our decision regarding our religious faith, thereby collecting a lot of empty yesterdays.

However, despite our natural hesitancies, the time does come when many of us do make the decision to leap. And, when we do, we should be prepared to give it our best. Apparently Philip didn't abandon himself completely to his decision. He tried to take the leap a little at a time, by degrees.

David Lloyd George once said, "Don't be afraid to take a big step. You can't cross a chasm in two small jumps." That describes us precisely; we try to cross a chasm in several small bounds.

There is a story about an elderly lady who had never ridden on an airplane. She needed to go from Houston to Atlanta. Her family was very concerned; they were afraid she would be so frightened that she might suffer a heart attack. When she arrived in Atlanta, several of her relatives were there to meet her. "Granny," they asked, "are you all right? Were you scared?" "No," she replied. "I was not scared at all, but I never put my whole weight down." Some people never put their whole weight down in their marriages, in their church loyalties, in their jobs, or in their interpersonal relationships. They hold back and they don't give their best. They don't make a total commitment; they don't abandon themselves. When we leap we should jump all the way, with total commitment, total abandon.

A clergyman colleague of mine tells a story that is doubtless apocryphal, but it emphasizes this truth. Prior to the beginning of a large church wedding, he, the groom, and the best man were out in the hall waiting for the ceremony to begin. The groom was unusually nervous and agitated. He kept pacing and wringing his hands. Finally, the minister became so concerned about him that he asked, "What's the matter, have you lost the ring?" "No, sir," the groom replied, "I've lost my enthusiasm."

One of our worst faults is to make a decision without enthusiasm; yet we Christians do that all the time. We just aren't excited about the leap; we do not give ourselves with total commitment.

Driving through a small Texas town one day, I saw an interesting sign in front of a church. The sign read, "Cold Corner Missionary Baptist Church." I've known a lot of churches with cold corners, but that's the first one that ever admitted it. That is what is wrong with the church and also with us. We are cold; we are not enthusiastic; we're not totally committed. The Bible says, "Would that you were either cold or hot." If we're going to leap, let's go all the way.

If we are to bring peace to the world we must go all the way; we must choose peace with total abandon. If we are to develop some sort of sanity in our society we must choose the ethical principles of Jesus Christ with total abandon. If we decide to become Christians we must choose it with total dedication.

Philip also teaches us not to look back. That's

another common fault; we make a choice and then we look back.

Clement of Alexandria, in A.D., 180 wrote that Philip was the disciple who, when called to follow Jesus, said, "Wait and let me bury my father." His father wasn't dead, but he would die some day. This person did not want to make a total commitment to Jesus until his father had died and he had been able to handle the estate, divide the property, and get everything in order. Jesus responded to him: "Leave the dead to bury their own dead." Strong words but accurate ones; once you leap, don't look back.

The children of Israel under Moses in the wilderness kept looking back. After a while they said: "Moses must not be leading us in the right direction. It wasn't so bad in Egypt after all. Maybe we ought to go back." They kept asking for another sign from God, pleading, "God, tell us that we're doing right. Send us a sign. Reassure us that our decision to follow Moses was right." They kept reconsidering.

That's also our problem as human beings. We make a decision and then we have afterthoughts. We accept a new job and think, "Maybe I shouldn't have made the move." We get married and think, "Perhaps I shouldn't have made this commitment."

How often have you said, "Maybe I made a

mistake. . . . Perhaps it was the wrong choice. . . . Maybe I shouldn't have done that"? Most of us do look back, and second-guessing is counterproductive to making our decisions work successfully. If we decide that we are going to be Christians, and then we start looking back, we are not going to know the abundance and joy of the Christian life.

Recently I had the privilege of hearing the great violinist Itzhak Perlman, and afterward had the pleasure of visiting with him. Suppose he had decided, after two or three years of playing the violin, that perhaps he had chosen the wrong instrument? What if he had thought that he really ought to be a trombone player or a clarinetist or a conductor? Part of the reason for his greatness is that once he made the decision to be a violinist he never looked back.

In the fourteenth chapter of John, Philip says, "Lord, show us the Father." He was looking back. He was saying, in effect: "Maybe this isn't the Messiah after all. Perhaps this isn't the Christ. Maybe we made the wrong decision. It wasn't too bad back there in Bethsaida with the horses after all." There may have been a trace of irritation in Jesus' voice when he answered him, "Philip, have you been so long with me and you still don't know, you still don't understand that I am in the Father and the Father is in me?"

Once we have the will and the courage to choose

the way of peace, then it will happen only if we don't look back. Once we in this country choose the way of a new morality in which the ethical principles of Jesus Christ become the basis for the actions of society, then we can't look back. Once we choose Jesus Christ as our Savior then we must not look back, because the success of the decision depends in part on our not doing so.

After the resurrection Philip was with the disciples when they gathered in the upper room. Now it appears that he was a totally committed, dedicated disciple. He had seen Jesus die. He had seen him crucified, and Jesus had risen from the grave to prove that the cross was not the end. Suddenly Philip was a devoted disciple of Christ. That must have been so, because a historian of the first century wrote that the disciple Philip had become one of the great spiritual lights of Asia. Tradition has it that Philip found martyrdom by being hanged on a hook on a tree, head down, opposite the temple at Hierapolis. Later, archaeologists uncovered an ancient inscription in the ruins of a building in Hierapolis, stating that the building is "the church of Philip the Apostle."

Finally, even hestitant Philip became a totally dedicated follower. Perhaps he became transformed when he saw Jesus die.

We've seen him die; you and I have seen him die. We've seen him crucified on a cross of society that cares nothing for justice and righteousness and human life. We've seen him die in a world of nations that continue to believe their differences can be settled by violence and war. We've seen him die in our own reluctance to accept him and follow him with total commitment, total abandon.

But, like Philip, if you've ever really seen him die, then you can never be the same again.

Scripture: Matthew 10:3; Mark 3:18; Luke 6:14; Acts 1:13; John 1:43-49; 6:5-7; 12:20-22; 14:8-12

What's in a Name?

THADDAEUS

CHAPTER

[3]

Names are very important, perhaps more significant than we realize because a name, by itself, can immediately elicit a powerful response—either positive or negative. For example, how do you feel when you hear the following: Napoleon. . . Socrates . . . Roosevelt . . . Churchill . . . Hitler . . . Mother Theresa . . . Shakespeare . . . Khomeini . . . Marilyn Monroe?

While Thaddaeus is the least known of all the disciples, one detail we do know about him is that he had three names. He was named Thaddaeus, Lebbaeus, and Judas. He is mentioned four times in scripture, once in each of the Gospels. In Matthew, Mark, and Luke, he is listed as a disciple. In John he asked Jesus a question. When Jesus was foretelling his death, saying, "After I am dead, the Holy Spirit will come and you will know more about me in death than you knew in life" (paraphrase), Thaddaeus asked a simple question, "Master, how is it that we can know more about you in death than in life?"

One of the reasons the name Judas might have been common in history was, perhaps, because of Judas Maccabaeus, who was one of the great heroes of the ancient Hebrews. It was once an honored name, but the name of Judas was disgraced when Judas Iscariot betrayed Jesus. That is why the Gospel writers refer to Thaddaeus as "Judas" (not Iscariot); they wanted everyone to know that this Judas was not Iscariot.

The Gospel writers were correct in making Thaddaeus' identity clear because names do affect us in life-changing ways and they affect others as well. As children, and sometimes as adults, we do great injury to ourselves and to others by assigning names to persons. We call someone Shorty or Slim or Fatso. When I was a little boy my mother would sometimes call me Sonny Boy. Until I was twelve years old, my father called me Little Man. Only in recent years have I forgiven him for that. Adult friends of my family would therefore also call me Little Man. That affected me adversely, and it colored their perception of me.

As a clergyman, I have been called Preacher by a few people. I dislike that designation, because they always make it sound like an infectious disease. Names do have an impact on us.

After the betrayal of Jesus by Judas Iscariot,

Thaddaeus doubtless was ashamed to admit that his name was Judas. It may be that the reason he is the least known of the disciples is that the Gospel writers wanted to protect him, hence their use of "Judas" (not Iscariot). Thaddaeus Judas was probably enormously affected by his name, and was aware that his name had a tremendous effect on others. We do need to be careful about the names we give to other people and the names we assume for ourselves.

Today, a vital question for us is, By what name are we called? The answer to that question is of great consequence because our name is an indication of our character, our morals, our ethics, our values, our priorities, and our life-style. Is our name generous? Are we called gracious, loving, unselfish? Or, are we called selfish, stingy, greedy, hateful? What is your name?

We would like our names to indicate that we are persons who work for peace and for the highest and best values in life. Our preference would be that our names suggest to the world that we are more interested in the quality of life than in the quantity of life. Yet, we live in a society where our value system is disarranged. We have put the highest dollars upon the cheapest values, and the cheapest dollars on those things that are most precious. Peace is of more value than war, but how much do we spend in America for peace? In recent years we have been spending $38,000 every hour for the hardware of war. What if we spent $38,000 every hour for the peaceful exploration of space, for the benefit of humanity, for the elimination of hunger, poverty, and inadequate housing? Surely, there is no doubt in the minds of each of us which value, which priority comes first—peace or war.

In our personal value systems the quality of life is surely of greater import than the quantity of life, but our efforts are directed primarily toward gaining quantity, not toward achieving more quality. And so our overaffluence, overabundance, and overindulgence, our permissive society with its "me only" syndrome, serve to diminish the quality of life.

This concern is being voiced not only by theologians, but by secularists as well. Recently, a professor of molecular biology at MIT, Jonathan King, was quoted as saying: "The value systems of American people are all mixed up. One reason is that the training of scientists and technologists tends to be focused in very narrow areas and they have no exposure to social and moral issues. Therefore, they attempt to reduce complex social issues to technological solutions. . . . We must fight for the basic values that impact the welfare of human beings."

In an article in *U.S. News & World Report* (July 5, 1982) a professor of psychology at the University of Colorado, John J. Conger, had this to say about the value system in America: "A primary value . . . may be a preoccupation with personal identity—the freedom to be yourself. This can . . . end up not as a self-realization but a trivial kind of self-indulgence."

Then Professor Conger goes on to say that in a world where " 'some get more and others get left out, and the hell with those who get left out,' I think then we're headed for a new version of the apocalypse."

What does that have to do with our name? Everything! For these values, these ethical, moral, and spiritual principles that impact society, that affect our desire for peace in the world, are most clearly enunciated in the teachings of Jesus Christ. People who claim the name of Jesus can make a difference in the world. "Therefore God has highly exalted him and bestowed on him the name which is above every name, that at the name of Jesus every knee should bow, in heaven and on earth and under the earth, and every tongue confess that Jesus Christ is Lord, to the glory of God the Father" (Phil. 2:9-11).

Could it be that Thaddaeus would have been willing to give up all of his names for the one name that indicated he was a follower of Jesus? Isn't that the best name that could be given to you and me? "He was a follower of Jesus; she was a Christian."

Gustave Doré, the artist, was once traveling through Europe. He came to the boundary of a country where he was required to show his passport. He searched through his pockets, but it was gone. "I've lost my passport," he explained to the guard, "but it's all right. I'm Doré, the artist. Please let me go through." "No, sir," the guard replied. "People come every day claiming to be someone they aren't. I cannot let you pass. Here is a pencil and paper. Draw me a picture so you can prove who you are."

For most of us our names prove who we are. How does your name identify you? Hopefully, we will come to understand the importance of the name by which we are called and to know that his name is above every name.

Scripture: Matthew 10:3; Mark 3:18; Luke 6:15-16; John 14:22

Surprised by God

NATHANIEL

CHAPTER

[4]

Many people believe in a mechanistic view of the universe. Even some Christians maintain that God created the world, "wound it up," and turned it loose. God, they conclude, is therefore inactive in history and the universe operates by inexorable axioms in which there are no surprises. However, there is a large body of testimony to the effect that God does surprise us. One of the disciples, the one known as Bartholomew or Nathaniel, was surprised by God.

There is a question as to whether this disciple's name was actually Bartholomew or Nathaniel. In the Synoptic Gospels and in the Book of Acts, one of the disciples is listed as Bartholomew. In the Gospel of John, he is listed as Nathaniel. Most scholars agree that this is the same disciple, that Bartholomew is the last name. We shall call him Nathaniel. He is identified as one of the seven to whom Jesus revealed himself at the Sea of Tiberias.

The second reference to him tells how Philip, having already become a disciple of Jesus, witnessed to Nathaniel by saying, "We have found him of whom Moses in the law and also the prophets wrote, Jesus of Nazareth." Nathaniel asked, "Can anything good come out of Nazareth?" "Come and see," Philip responded. They walked toward Jesus and when Jesus saw them coming, he said, "Behold, an Israelite, indeed, in whom is no guile!" "How do you know about me?" Nathaniel asked. And Jesus responded, "I saw you under the fig tree."

The fig tree was a symbol for peace. Devout Jews stood or sat under its shady branches to pray, meditate, and express their devotion to God. Jesus assumed, and rightly so, that Nathaniel was praying; he might have been asking God to send the Messiah. Jesus knew that here was a good man, a pure man, a righteous man. Nathaniel, evidently, was so impressed by the fact that Jesus could see within his heart and soul that he was immediately converted, and proclaimed, "You are the Son of God. You are the King of Israel."

We might wonder why Nathaniel asked, "Can anything good come out of Nazareth?" He lived in Cana which was a small town eight miles north of Nazareth. We might assume that there was a football rivalry between the two communities. Maybe the year before Nazareth had beaten Cana, and

Nathaniel held a grudge because of that. On the other hand, he may have been correct about Nazareth. Maybe it was a village of loose morals and questionable reputation. If you have ever been there, you know it is not a very impressive city even today.

Nathaniel was surprised by God because out of Nazareth came the Savior of the world. We, too, are often surprised. We are surprised by people, places, events, and history. There is a keen rivalry between Houston and Dallas, our little suburb up north. We sometimes wonder if anything good can come out of Dallas. And, our children rapidly imitate our bias.

Not long ago, a six-year-old boy in Houston prayed, "God bless Mommy and Daddy and little sister, and bless my puppy dog. And I guess, God, this is good-bye, because tomorrow we're moving to Dallas."

We, too, are often surprised that good can come out of a person or a place or an event or history. We say, "This is a good day in history," or, "This is a bad day." Later, in retrospect, history may prove us wrong; the good day may have been a bad day and the bad day may have been a good day. We say about our life, "This is an uneventful day," or, "This is an exciting day." Looking back, the exciting day may have really been uneventful and the seemingly dull day may have been ultimately significant.

In my entire ministry, I've only had one unhappy appointment. It was in the early days of my career when the bishop asked me to go to a little church. I have never known before or since a church like that one. While there I decided to propose something that everyone in the congregation could agree on. It seemed to me that surely there could be no dissent about having a revival meeting but I was wrong. They voted against it.

I remember thinking to myself, "This is the worst time in my life. I am the pastor of a congregation that cannot even agree to have a revival meeting." But, in retrospect, I'm surprised to understand that it was one of the best times of my life, a time of learning and growing. You see, we're often surprised because we misjudge a situation.

We make the same mistake in regard to people. There was a president whom I once thought was the worst president America ever had, but now both history and I understand that he was one of the best chief executives our country has ever had. We are constantly surprised. Nathaniel teaches us that life, events, places, people, history are not always as they seem to be.

We're often also surprised by God. Several months ago the baptism of a baby was scheduled to be held in the chapel. The family was waiting when I arrived. The couple's four-year-old son was sitting on the steps leading to the altar. I sat down next to him and began to talk to him. "What is your name?" I asked. "How old are you?" The little boy had a wonderful personality, he was very articulate, and he was an especially beautiful child with huge sparkling blue eyes. Finally, I asked, "Where did you get those big beautiful blue eyes?" For a moment he was taken by surprise, then he said, "I don't know; God just popped 'em in!"

We are surprised that God can create incredible human beings like you and me. Continually, God does keep surprising us in many experiences of life. In fact, the Old Testament is partially a story of God's surprises. God called Moses to lead the Israelites and, in effect, Moses replied, "God, I can't do that! You've picked the wrong person." But God said, "Yes, you can," and Moses did as he was instructed. He was surprised by God. Samuel heard a voice calling him; he thought it was Eli, the priest. He did not expect it to be God's voice, but it was. He, too, was surprised by God.

The New Testament is also in part the story of God's surprises. Jesus said, "I have come not to destroy the law but to fulfill the law. It has been said of old in the law 'an eye for an eye and a tooth for a tooth,' but I say to you, love your enemies" (paraphrase). Surprise, surprise! Jesus' enemies tried to trick him by asking, "To whom do you pay tribute, Caesar or God?" Then came the unexpected as Jesus answered, "Pay to Caesar that which belongs to Caesar; pay to God that which belongs to God." Peter betrayed Jesus at the worst possible moment, when Jesus was on trial for his life; how astonishing it is that Peter was chosen to preach the sermon at Pentecost at which three thousand people were added to the church. How God does surprise us!

Surprises happen in our individual lives. When he was fifteen years old, the evangelist Charles Spurgeon started to church one Sunday. There was a blizzard and the heavily falling snow made the road impassable. He couldn't get to his church, but he saw a little church building down a side street. It was a Primitive Methodist Church which he had never attended. He made his way to the church and joined the fifteen people who were there. The pastor didn't arrive because of the blizzard, so a layman in the congregation took over the service. For the sermon, the layman announced as his text, "Look unto me and be ye saved, all the ends of the earth." Charles Spurgeon later reported that the text was apparently all the layman knew. He kept repeating, "Look unto me and be ye saved, all the ends of the earth." Then, he would try to elaborate, but evidently he couldn't think of anything more to say, so he would repeat the text again. Over and over he intoned, "Look unto me and be ye saved, all the ends of the earth." It became rather ludicrous until the layman spotted Charles Spurgeon sitting there. He said, "Young man, you look miserable, and you'll always be miserable. Miserable in life and miserable in death unless you obey my text. Young man, look to Jesus. Look, look, look!" Charles Spurgeon wrote, "I looked and suddenly the cloud was gone. The darkness was rolled away and for the first time in my life I saw the sun." What a surprise on that bleak winter day!

A similar event occurred in the life of Sir Wilfred Grenfell when he was a medical student in London. One day, while he was on his way to call on a patient, he saw a large tent where Dwight Moody was holding a revival. Strictly out of curiosity Wilfred Grenfell went into the tent. He was appalled at what was going on. Then someone called on a member of the congregation to pray. The man prayed and prayed, for five minutes; his prayer lengthened to ten minutes. By this time young Wilfred Grenfell had had enough. He rose to walk out, but just as he did so, Dwight Moody said, "While the brother continues his prayer, let's all sing a hymn." That struck a chord in Wilfred Grenfell's mind, and he thought, "If religion is like that, I'm going to stay," and he sat down again. By the end of the service, Wilfred Grenfell had been surprised by God. He went away thinking, "I will vow to be the kind of doctor Christ would be or else I will abandon Christianity altogether."

God surprised Nathaniel because out of Nazareth came the Savior of the world, and God surprises us, too. Maybe Nathaniel's concept of God was too limited. His God was too small; that may be our problem also. Perhaps we need to enlarge our concept of God. We perceive of God in the finite role of our own limited understanding and adhere to the ideas that represent our human intellectual grasp. When we do that, we reduce God to our size, we even sometimes make him an anthropomorphic God who has hands, arms, and feet as we do, thus destroying our capacity to understand that God is God.

In an interview Ernest Hemingway said, "My God has painted wonderful pictures, written some fine books, fought Napoleon's rear guard action in the retreat from Moscow, battled on both sides in the American Civil War, done away with yellow fever, taught Picasso how to draw, Jim Thorpe how to play football, sired Citation, and killed George Armstrong Custer." That makes the point both graphic and memorable.

We need to reintroduce the awe, the wonder, the mystery, and the greatness of God. That is why I deplore the current tendency among some Christians who equate God and Christ. They pray to Christ: "O Christ, O Jesus." They talk about Jesus and Christ in their prayer and never mention God.

The temptation to exalt Jesus at the expense of God is wrong because Jesus was divine but God is never human. God is God.

W. B. J. Martin told about a minister who preached a sermon on astronomy one Sunday every year. After two or three years, his young associate asked, "Why do you preach a sermon on astronomy each year? It doesn't have anything to do with the Bible or the Christian faith." The minister replied, "To enlarge our concept of God." That is a very good idea. We ought to have a few sermons each year that remind us of the mystery of the inexplicable God.

Affirmation is sometimes more desirable than explanation. That is why I am grateful for the hymns, the creeds, and the liturgy; they just affirm, they don't explain. Occasionally, someone asks, "Would you explain this phrase?" This question indicates that the person is missing the point altogether. At times we are not supposed to understand, but simply affirm because that gives us the opportunity to proclaim the wonder, the awe, and the adoration.

There was a scholar who spent literally all of his working life studying the Gospel of John. He rarely consulted another book of the Bible; he never pondered another scriptural phrase. As he reached the end of a long life, he said, "I still don't understand it; I still don't understand the Gospel of

John." Indeed, he didn't nor do we because God is God.

All of our human attributes are dim reflections of God, but they are very dim reflections. Consider the quality of love. Our human love is a reflection of God's love. For someone has truly said that if you multiply a mother's love by infinity, you have only touched the outer fringe of God's love for the worst person who ever lived in the world. That puts our understanding in proper perspective, doesn't it? And, it makes us realize that trying to explain God is like dipping up the ocean with a teacup. Nathaniel can teach us that we need to enlarge our concept of God. He should not have been surprised that God brought the Savior of the world out of the little town of Nazareth and we, too, need to learn to expect God's surprises—in our lives, in the world, and in the church.

Someone said, "Attempt great things for God; expect great things from God." Note that we have to attempt great things for God before we can expect great things from God. We have to make a resolute attempt to bring peace to the world. We must attempt to change the moral and ethical climate in society before we can expect great things from God. We must try to raise the consciousness of value identification among all people. We must attempt to find answers for the hunger, poverty, and injustice of the world. When we make the valiant effort we can expect surprises from God.

Rainer Maria Rilke wrote:

> He is the water; you need only mould
> the cup out of two hands extended yonder;
> and if you kneel as well, why, then he'll squander
> and pass all your capacity to hold.

Indeed, God pours out more blessings than we're able to hold when we attempt great things for him.

"Can anything good come out of Nazareth?" That's not the right question. The right question is, Can anything good come out of your city, your church? Can anything good come out of your life and mine?

Scripture: Matthew 10:3; Mark 3:18; Luke 6:14; Acts 1:13; John 1:45-49; 21:2

Feet of Clay

JOHN

CHAPTER

[5]

Two of the disciples may have been cousins of Jesus, James and John. Zebedee, John's father, was a prosperous fisherman in Bethsaida who owned his own vessels. John himself was a successful fisherman-businessman before he became a disciple. John's mother was at the cross when Christ was crucified, and was one of the women who anointed Christ's body with sweet spices.

John was the younger brother of James, and the youngest of all the disciples. He was a member of Jesus' inner cabinet, the triumvirate of Peter, James and John. From his writings we might conclude that John had the best mind of all of the disciples. He was always there; he sat next to Christ at the Last Supper, he was at Christ's trial, and he was present at the crucifixion, perhaps the only disciple present. In the post-resurrection appearance of Jesus at the Sea of Galilee, John was also there. He was entrusted with the care of Jesus' mother, the most supreme compliment that Jesus could pay him. He wrote the Gospel of John, the three epistles of John, and, in the cave on the isle of Patmos, he wrote the Book of Revelation.

Charles R. Brown reminds us that there are three perceptions of John.

1. He may be perceived first of all as the John of legend and art. Many of the portraits of John exhibit a marked similarity in that they show him with an expression of tenderness, softness, and delicacy. The viewer often finds an air of mysticism about him. He is always portrayed without a beard. That may be a misconception, based on the artist's understanding of John as being the beloved disciple, the disciple of love.

2. The second perception is the John of the early gospels, the John who had feet of clay. The Bible calls James and John "sons of thunder." That is a deserved title because John was hot-tempered, impetuous, bombastic, exclusive, and ambitious. He was selfish, undisciplined, prejudiced, and intolerant. He was a radical from the word go. According to scripture, James and John once saw a man casting out demons and they stopped him, they forbade him. Then they rushed to Jesus, probably bursting with self-righteousness, and said, "Master, we saw a man casting out demons in your name and we forbade him because he does not follow with us" (Luke 9:49). Jesus rebuked them

saying, "Do not forbid him; for he that is not against you is for you" (verse 50).

On another occasion, scripture is unclear at this point, either James and John, or their mother, wanted them to sit at the right and left hand of Jesus. The request was that when Jesus' kingdom came one would sit at his right hand and the other at his left hand. Even the other disciples were repelled by such raw, greedy ambition. Another time, because certain Samaritans denied them hospitality, James and John wanted the inhabitants of that entire village burned to death.

As always, there is a lesson to be learned, even from John, the son of thunder. If John could make it as a disciple, so can we. If Jesus could use him, he can use us. If John could be transformed into the "beloved disciple," so can we.

There are people who say, "I can't be a Christian. I'm not good enough. I can't join the church until I'm a better person." A man once told me that he couldn't join the church because he had committed the unforgivable sin. The only unforgivable sin that I know of is the sin of believing that there is a sin God cannot forgive. Remember that John had feet of clay, but Jesus chose him, accepted him, used him, and transformed him.

3. The third perception is the John of the later gospels when divine grace had done its work. Then we see him not as the son of thunder, but we see

him as a mature, converted, transformed Christian, when his bombastic, aggressive personality has been tamed by the love of Christ; when his sharp, quick mind has been impregnated with a new understanding of the Good News of Christ in all of its nuances. John learned that Christ's kingdom is not a political kingdom, but a spiritual one.

There is a fine line between the sinner and the saint. We see John first as a sinner, and then as a saint. The same personality, the same characteristics that made John a son of thunder with feet of clay also serve to make him an authentic follower of Christ. A fine line also exists between a successful criminal and a successful Christian. The qualities that make a really good sinner are the same qualities that make a really good saint. A strong personality, high motivation, and courage are needed by both. For instance, the most nefarious figures in history might have been outstanding Christians if their skills, talents, and highly motivated personalities had been used for Christ.

Saul of Tarsus, a persecutor of the Christians, became Saint Paul, the great missionary of the church. John, the son of thunder, became the redeemed child of God with a heart of love. He was transformed by Christ and he writes of this experience in I John 3:2: "We are God's children now; it does not yet appear what we shall be, but we know that when he appears we shall be like him." In addition, he writes of the transforming power of God's love: "For God so loved the world. . . . God is love and he who abides in love, abides in God and God abides in him. . . . Let us love one another for God is love and he who loves is born of God and knows God, and he who does not love does not know God and God does not know him. . . . In this is love, not that we loved God, but that he loves us and sent his son to be the expiation for our sins."

Most of us do not have the slightest notion of the power of God's love, or even a dim conception of the power of human love. In James Thurber's contemporary fable, "The White Deer," a beautiful princess comes under the spell of a witch who transforms her into a white deer. The king and his three sons are out hunting one day and they see the white deer. They start to shoot it, but, just at that moment, she turns back into a human princess. They take her back to their castle with them. However, she is unable to remember where she came from or who she is. The court psychiatrist tries to help her remember by delving into her past, but he is unsuccessful. So, the court philosopher tries to help her regain her memory, but his efforts are also in vain. Finally, it is revealed that the only way she can remember is to receive a love that will not fail. In the fable, the youngest of the king's sons bestows that love upon her, a love that will not fail; then she remembers where she came from and who she is. The power of love, even human love, can work miracles mentally, emotionally, spiritually, and, at times, physically.

The famous clergyman Theodore Parker Ferris wrote of a time when he visited a leper colony in Africa. One day he watched a nurse dress bleeding sores on the leg of an old man. Theodore Parker Ferris was not a naïve person who lived in an ivory tower, insulated from the real world. Although he had seen many terrible things, he said that was the worst sight he had ever seen. "It was repulsive, revolting, gruesome," he said, "and before she had finished I almost became ill." When she had completed the dressing, he said to her, "I wouldn't do that for $10,000!" The nurse replied, "Neither would I."

But for love she would, and for love she did. The ultimate hope of the world is to understand and accept the redemptive, transforming power of God's love. God's love, in its divinest dimension, transformed John.

Legend has it that John lived to be one hundred years old. The story is told that in his later years he spent his time teaching young Christians. He taught them about love every day until, finally, one of his students said to him, "John, isn't there something you can tell us, other than love?" "There is nothing else," John replied, "just love, love, love."

What Christ did for John, he can do for us. God can take us as we are and change us by his love made manifest in Jesus Christ. That's what we need more than anything else because for us also, there is nothing else—just love, love, love.

Scripture: Mark 10:35-45

Saint and Sinner
JAMES

CHAPTER

[6]

James was the older brother of John, and the son of Zebedee and Salome. Tradition has it that Salome was the sister of the Virgin Mary, therefore James and Jesus may have been first cousins. James, like his father, was a prosperous fisherman until he was called to be a disciple. Though he was selected to be a part of the triumvirate of Peter, James, and John, James was the quiet one of the three. He was the silent member, showing signs of both introversion and introspection. Yet, he was vociferous enough to participate with his brother in asking for permission to burn the Samaritan village and all the inhabitants therein because they refused hospitality to Jesus. It seems obvious that he, along with John, was also a son of thunder because of his temper, his anger. His unreasoned ambition is evidenced by the request that he sit at the right or the left hand of Jesus, in effect, wanting to be the prime minister or secretary of state. This appeal incurred the anger of the other disciples.

James' weak points are also ours. As we often do, he failed to understand Jesus. James expressed his love, loyalty, and commitment to Jesus in the wrong way. He doubtless thought that Jesus was going to establish an earthly kingdom, a political empire. He simply did not understand. But, at last, James became the disciple Jesus knew he could become. And, it is in this process that he teaches us some very valuable lessons.

First of all, we learn from James that like him we are all mixtures of good and evil. All of us are Dr. Jekylls and Mr. Hydes. James wanted to burn the village and its inhospitable inhabitants. He wanted to be the prime minister, yet he also loved Jesus and was committed to him. Paul thoroughly understood this problem in our nature when he wrote, "The things I want to do, I don't do; and the things I don't want to do, I do" (paraphrase).

All of us are familiar with that experience. There is a part of us that never seems to get converted. James had trouble getting his anger converted; he had difficulty getting his ambition converted. We, too, have a part or parts of us that often are not converted. Cassius asked Brutus, "Is that you, my Lord?" The reply was, "A part of me." Isn't that also true of you and me? A portion of us never gets converted; sometimes it's our attitude or our temper, oftentimes it's our pocketbook. All of us are unique mixtures of saint and sinner.

When Leonardo da Vinci was painting the *Last Supper,* he looked for a person who could pose as a model for Jesus Christ. He found an angelic faced young man who sang in the choir in the Milan Cathedral, and he used him as a model to paint the face of Jesus. Many years later, da Vinci was looking for a model for a sinner. One day, while walking the streets of Rome, he saw a man. The man's face vividly portrayed vice, greed, dissipation, and he asked him to pose. When they reached his studio, da Vinci asked the man his name. "Oh, you know me," the man replied. "I posed for your painting of the Last Supper." Good and bad, Dr. Jekylls and Mr. Hydes, saints and sinners; that's who we are. All of us are a mixture of both good and evil.

We have a tendency to forget that God made us this way. He could have made us perfect; he could have made us incapable of greed or vice or anger. But he would have been less than God had he done so. He would have been a divine puppeteer who pulled the strings and forced us to do his will, thereby robbing us of the power of choice.

When we affirm in Christian doctrine that we are made in the image of God, that we have the spark of God's own divinity, that means that God made us free moral agents. We can think, reason, decide, choose, and commit for ourselves. To be made in the image of God means that you and I can say, "I am . . . I can . . . I ought . . . I will." Whatever else we believe about God, whatever else we believe about the universe or about human beings, we know we are free moral agents.

I hear people say things about God, about human beings, and about God's work and actions in the world that are not true because they are a denial of this truth. God bestowed upon us the stamp of his own image and that makes us free moral agents, able to choose for ourselves. God does not coerce us, does not force us, does not interfere with that divine right to make our own choices.

The Jews well understood the duality within us, and called our two natures Yetser Hatob and Yetser Hara. Paul also certainly understood. He said the right and wrong within us was like two men inside one body pulling in different directions; a split personality, a spiritual schizophrenia. This does not occur because of the intervention of another god into human life who wars with God over which one is going to take command. Not at all. This is the gift of God himself who made us a mixture of good and evil by giving to us his own divinity; the ability to reason, to choose, and to decide for ourselves. If God had done otherwise, he would not be God because had he forced us, then there would be no virtue available for us. But God gave us the right to choose, so that we can elect to grow and to become in his likeness.

We are also so made that the intuition for good is greater than the intuition for evil. You may hear people say, "Man is primarily evil. Human beings are evil for the most part." That is not true. The intuition for good is definitely greater than the intuition for evil.

In the Metropolitan Museum of Art in New York City, there is a white marble statue called *The Struggle Between the Two Natures,* by George Grey Barnard. It depicts two identical male figures. One is lying on the ground while the other stands over him with one foot on his thigh and the other foot on his neck. They look like wrestlers with every muscle clearly visible. This piece of sculpture symbolizes the struggle between our spiritual instinct and our survival instinct. The artist does not make the judgment; he leaves the judgment to the viewer.

In that respect, the artist is incorrect because that is not the truth. The truth is the deck is stacked. We are not equally good and evil. While God made us with freedom to choose the evil, "God has made us for Himself and our hearts are restless until we find rest in Him." We are tipped in the direction of God and the instinct for good is stronger than the instinct for evil.

Thomas Merton, the great mystic, once asked, "How did it ever happen that, when the dregs of the world had collected in western Europe, when the Goths and the Franks and the Normans and the Lombards had mingled with the rot of old Rome to form a patchwork of hybrid races, all notable for ferocity, hatred, stupidity, craftiness, lust and brutality—how did it happen that from all of this, there should come the Gregorian chant, cathedrals, the poems of Prudentius, the commentaries and histories of Bede, St. Augustine's *City of God*?" We can answer that question. It happened because human beings, by their very divine nature, are tilted in the direction of good and God. "God has made us for Himself and our hearts are restless until we find rest in Him."

James also teaches us that the way to good and God is through Jesus Christ. We know that. Having been given the instinct for good, we yearn for something that is better. We try to find that which is better in many ways: in knowledge, in science, in material possessions, in social status, or in the exercise of the human will, by vowing, "I will be good; I will, I will, I will!" Or, we try to find it in esoteric answers such as astrology, horoscopes, yoga, or the Eastern mystery religions. But it is never found in any of those areas. Paul Tournier said, "Man left to himself is lost. Our own efforts, our own virtue, our own good will and good intentions cannot banish our disease." Indeed not.

Bertrand Russell kept searching for the realization of the best within him. He said, "The center of myself is always eternally a terrible pain searching for something beyond which the world contains. I do not find it. I do not think it is to be found, but the love of it is my life." Oh, if he had only searched a little farther he would have discovered that finally, ultimately, we are found or we find the grace of God in Jesus Christ to be the answer to our instinct for good. Sir James Simpson, the Scottish surgeon, said, "My greatest discovery is that I am a great sinner and that Jesus is a great Savior."

Indeed, many of us have started on the road as James did, by accepting Jesus Christ as the way, but like James, that isn't enough. James had accepted Christ. He had committed himself with love and loyalty, but that wasn't enough either because—and perhaps this is the most important thing that James teaches us—becoming a mature Christian takes time, effort, work and study. You can become an instantaneous follower of Jesus Christ. In the turning of a thought and the twinkling of an eye, you can become a follower of Jesus Christ. But, you cannot become an instantaneous Christian, that is, in the finished, complete, mature sense of Christianity.

James loved Jesus. He was loyal, courageous, committed, and he had given Jesus the utmost of his intellectual and spiritual capacity, but James was not a finished Christian yet. He was not a completed Christian. He was a son of thunder with an uncontrollable temper. He was willing to burn a village and kill people in the name of Jesus Christ. He wanted to sit at the right hand of Jesus and be the prime minister. He was a follower of Christ, but he was not a mature, finished, completed Christian. Total conversion is not instantaneous and it is not irrevocable.

Frederick Buechner has pointed out that the alphabet of grace has no vowels, not because God tries to obscure his way, but because each of us has to fill in the vowels ourselves. The word must become incarnate in us individually and separately according to *our* faith, *our* understanding, and *our* spiritual growth. That takes time, it takes understanding, it takes perception, it takes study to be able to insert our vowels into the alphabet of grace and to incarnate his word into our daily living.

That's why we always have to continue fighting the instinct for evil; why we always have to struggle up the hill and why we falter and fall back. That's why we need to read and study and participate in corporate worship with like-minded Christians. Otherwise, we never become completed, finished Christians.

There are some people who don't even know they don't know. They belong to a church. They attend most Sundays, they put their offerings in, and they think they are completed Christians. But doing that and that alone is not enough.

A lady once called me and said, "I wish you had it!" I told her that I didn't understand what she was saying. "I wish you had what I have," she insisted. I repeated that I didn't understand. She explained by saying, "You really don't have Christianity like I do." I asked, "Does that mean you're perfect?" "It means that I have been totally and completely sanctified," she replied. "Every part of me is totally sanctified, therefore I have no evil instincts or intentions or thoughts."

That reminds me of Dr. Clarence Forsberg's story about two fellows who were sitting on a park bench. One asked the other, "What's your name?" He said, "Napoleon Bonaparte." "Who gave you that name?" "God did." The first man said, "I did not!"

James was not God and we are not God. However, James realized that he wasn't God. He knew that he was not a completed, finished, mature Christian. And so, he listened, he learned, he prayed, he studied, and he grew until, in Acts 12:1-2, we read: "Herod the king laid violent hands upon some who belonged to the church. He killed James the brother of John with the sword." James, saint and sinner that he was, finally became the disciple whom Jesus knew he could become. In fact, he became a Christian martyr, killed by the sword because of his faith.

We, you and I, are very much like James. We're a mixture of good and evil, but our instinct is for good. Most of us, perhaps all of us, have been found by the grace of God in Jesus Christ, and what we need now is to spend the effort and time to study, learn, and search until we can grow into the fullness of the likeness of God in Jesus Christ. I pray that all of us will join the struggle and make the effort to climb the hill that leads us to his cross and to ours.

Scripture: Mark 10:35-41; Acts 12:1-2

Believing Through Doubt
THOMAS

CHAPTER

[7]

All of us, to some degree or another, have difficulty with our doubts. Some of us adamantly refuse to admit that we have any, while others live in a make-believe world pretending to understand when we do not. The latter are those who are ashamed of their uncertainties and feel guilty, therefore they are reluctant to voice their skepticism. They are fearful that they will be thought ignorant, so they feign understanding.

For those of us who feel uncomfortable with our doubt, there is instruction in the experience of the disciple Thomas. Historically, we think of him primarily as "Doubting Thomas," overlooking the fact that he was courageous, committed, and had great love for Jesus Christ. When Jesus heard that Lazarus, his very dear friend, was desparately ill, he said, "I need to go to him." But the disciples, knowing that Bethany was a place where Jesus' enemies were concentrated and that he might be killed, did not want him to go and did not want to go with him. It was Thomas who said, "Let us go and die with him." He was the only disciple who was willing to go with Jesus, thereby risking his own life.

Jesus' crucifixion was exactly what Thomas had anticipated. He possessed the insight to know that Jesus' words and deeds were of such a revolutionary nature as to inevitably result in his crucifixion. But, although he had expected it, the death of Jesus left Thomas brokenhearted and grief-stricken; he went into solitude, away from the other disciples, to grieve alone. Some of us also have chosen to suffer alone. For whatever reason, we opt to bear our grief by ourselves, isolated even from those who love us.

For Thomas, the news of the resurrection was too good to be true. He protested, "That can't be! I will never believe unless I see the nail prints in his hands and feel the spearmark in his side" (paraphrase). He became known as Doubting Thomas because he could not believe the word of the resurrection.

Perhaps Jesus knew who Thomas was before he chose him as a disciple. Jesus may have been aware that Thomas had an analytical, candid, inquiring mind. Most of us also realize that it is beneficial to have one person in a group who is always asking questions and demanding answers. We learn from Thomas that it is okay to doubt.

Thomas was totally honest in his response to the news of the resurrection, refusing to pretend that he understood or saying that he believed when he did not. He would not be dishonest about his faith, about his creed.

Some time ago a lady called me, and said, "I am ninety years old. I have belonged to the church all of my life. I have always believed everything the church has taught me, everything in the Bible. Now, I'm so ashamed; I feel so guilty, but at ninety years of age I am finally doubting the existence of God. Isn't that awful?" "No," I assured her, "I think that's fine. I do the same thing. Every few days I have some reason to doubt the existence of God. Tell me about it." After we talked for a while, she said that she felt better for having confessed her doubt, and she was appreciative because someone had given her permission to doubt.

We express our doubt in varying ways. At times our doubt is expressed with anger and hostility. These are legitimate, acceptable expressions of our honest inquiry and should not make us feel guilty. Looking back over my own ministry, some experiences come to mind that produced doubt and anger: a four-year-old girl killed by a drunken driver; a teenage suicide; an entire family of five dead as the result of a car accident; a man who lost everything.

Some years ago a child died in a senseless accident. Someone called to inform me of her death, and I rushed to be with her parents. When I arrived at their home, her mother opened the door and, when she saw me, she said, "Go away. I don't want to see you. There is no God!" She tried to close the door in my face, but I would not let her. Finally, I was able to affirm her anger and convince her that it was okay to be angry with God. Later, she was able to move into a more profound understanding of God's nature. I believe that God can understand and appreciate the honest, candid mind that railed in anger at such injustice.

Like Job, all of us, at one time or another, want to cry out, "Oh, that I knew where I might find him" (Job 23:3). At other times we may feel like Elijah thinking, I, even I only, am left" (I Kings 19:10). When inexplicable tragedies happen to us, God understands our doubts, our questions, and even our anger.

Not only is it okay to doubt, but it is tempting to say that it is necessary because, for one thing, doubt can lead us to knowledge. Most of the progress in the world is due to doubt. Because man doubted that a heavier than air machine could fly, the airplane was invented. Doubt motivated the technology that enabled man to go to the moon.

Doubt lead Thomas to the knowledge of the resurrected Christ. Because of his doubts, Thomas was allowed to touch the nail prints and feel the spearmark, and thus be convinced that Christ had truly conquered the grave.

Furthermore, doubt can give us understanding. Knowledge without understanding is useless, is it not? Our generation is probably the most knowledgeable generation that ever lived; we have access to more information. However, we often do not understand the facts we possess or know how to prioritize the value of this information. That's why society is in chaos. Knowledge without understanding, facts without value identification result in a lack of moral and ethical strength.

Corporate society has become an accomplice to the same error. Every college graduate knows that the best jobs and the largest salaries go to the applicants whose grades have placed them in the top tenth of their graduating class. Rather than stressing academic achievement only, shouldn't we also ask students if they intend to make some compensating contribution to society, if they have a sense of social justice, and if they subscribe to moral and ethical values that will result in a better life for themselves and others? The provost of a major university recently wrote me, "Most of the ills of our society, moral and ethical, are caused by the fact that universities have taught knowledge without understanding and values."

Many of our universities appear to be almost totally committed to providing factual knowledge for their students without a corresponding effort to provide understanding and meaning. The result is students who have knowledge without understanding and facts without value identification.

In the business and corporate world we need to doubt some things. In higher education we need to doubt some things. In the church we need to doubt some things; we need to doubt some creeds, doctrines, beliefs, and easy clichés. We need to call some points into question, to ask, to be skeptical, inquisitive, and curious. We need understanding and one way we get it is through our doubts.

It is also true that doubt can lead us to faith. The opposite of faith is despair, not doubt. Doubt is a friend of faith. It is doubt that enables our faith to grow and to know and to understand the faith that we profess.

Frederick Buechner wrote, "If you don't have any doubts you are either kidding yourself or you're sound asleep. Doubts are the ants in the pants of faith. They keep it awake and moving." It certainly is true that doubts keep the thinking process alive. They keep us moving, searching, seeking, asking questions, being inquisitive, so that the faith we finally possess will be ours.

We can move from doubt to faith by questioning our doubts. Doubt enables us to ask questions and seek answers which cause us to question our-doubts. Thus we may return to faith by the road of doubt.

If Thomas had not doubted, he would never have believed that Jesus had truly arisen from the dead. Thomas had gone into solitude with his grief but that was a mistake, because when Jesus appeared after the resurrection Thomas wasn't there. Eight days later Jesus appeared again, and this time Thomas was there. Jesus already knew of his doubt and so he said, "Touch me, and see for yourself" (paraphrase). Thomas did, and then he confessed his faith, "My Lord and my God!" Yet, he came to that faith through doubt.

There was once a teenager who had always been a believer, a dedicated Christian, and an active member of the church. Suddenly, a time came when she was beset by doubts. She doubted that God really existed. She doubted that Jesus Christ was the Savior of the world; she doubted the truth of the Bible. She felt so guilty. Ashamed of her skepticism, she did not want to share her doubts with her parents, who were committed Christians. Instead, she went to an older lady who was a friend of her mother's. With great embarrassment, the girl said, "Suddenly, I'm not sure there is a God. I'm not sure there is a Christ." After she had talked for a while, the lady said, "Why don't you tell me about your doubts? Try to prove your doubts to me." So, the girl started to try to prove that there was no God. After a few sentences, she couldn't think of anything else to say. As she tried to explain her disbelief, she discovered that it was harder not to believe than to believe. Trying to prove her doubts enabled her to prove her faith. When the conversation was over, she was able to say, "I do believe." That faith was then hers by possession, not by inheritance. She came to faith through doubt.

Some of us feel doubt and we are ashamed and guilty because we do. The lesson of Thomas is that it is okay to doubt. Doubt can lead us to knowledge, to understanding, and to faith. May God make it so for each one of us.

Scripture: John 11:16; 20:24-29

Instant Acceptance
MATTHEW

CHAPTER

[8]

Everybody needs a purpose in life. God has so made us that we must have a reason for living. We have to have an inner dynamic, an interior motivation. The psychiatrist Viktor Frankl wrote: "If you have a 'why' you can live with any 'what.' " That fact became clear to Dr. Frankl as he observed prisoners in concentration camps during World War II. The prisoners, he discovered, could survive almost any *what* if they had a *why.* Those who did not have a *why* to live could not survive the *what* of prison life. That is also true of our human condition; we have to have a cause outside ourselves.

Matthew, called Levi by Mark and Luke, was a publican, which means tax gatherer. He had sold out to Rome, the conquering country, and agreed to collect taxes from his fellow countrymen. In ancient Palestine that was the way to get rich, because a tax collector could keep all the money he collected over the amount due Rome. That is why tax collectors, at that time, were called "leeches," and why they were enemies of society and the synagogue. The tax collector stole from his own people. In order to do that, he had to be cold, calculating, and heartless.

Matthew sat at the toll booth at Capernaum. Jesus and his mother had moved to Capernaum, and doubtless Jesus had gone into the toll booth to pay his mother's taxes. In all probability it was there that he and Matthew came to know each other. Jesus must have believed that there was something good in Matthew. Maybe he thought Matthew could be as successful at the kingdom of God as he was at extortion. So, one day Jesus went into the toll booth and simply said to Matthew, "Follow me." Amazingly, Matthew got up and followed Jesus. He didn't wait to put on his coat, he didn't clean off his desk, gather his personal effects, or turn in an official resignation. No questions, no hesitancy, no quibbling; it was instant acceptance.

Apparently, Matthew needed to believe. Can you imagine how it must have been to spend your day extorting and cheating poor people, widows and, literally, taking bread out of the mouths of children, for no other reason than to increase your own bank account? Can you imagine the guilt, the shame, and the uselessness he felt leading that kind of existence, with no purpose or meaning? Matthew certainly seems to have needed a *why* in his life. However, you don't have to be a scoundrel to feel that your life lacks a purpose. Many people find life boring and meaningless because they have no inner motivation. They really have no reason to get up in the morning. Clothes to wear, food to eat, and money to spend are in ample supply; but that is not enough. Life remains bleak and purposeless for them.

A young man in another city, who inherited a large fortune, has no wife, no children, no family, and no job. He does not have to work. His life is fraught with fear and insecurity lest what he has will be taken from him. That young man has no cause outside himself. He is miserable, wretched, and unhappy. If he could find Christ then he would discover purpose and joy in his life. Sara Henderson Hay expressed this thought poetically:

> It is a piteous thing to be
> Enlisted in no cause at all,
> Unsworn to any heraldry,
> To fly no banner from the wall,
> Own nothing you would sweat or try for,
> Or bruise your hands, or bleed, or die for.

It is more tragic than we can imagine to have nothing you would bleed or die for. Matthew had a job, he had a marvelous income, he had security, but his life had no meaning. He needed a cause outside of himself; he needed to believe.

He was also evidently ready to believe. He had learned what some people never learn; that is, there comes a time when we decide that what we have is not enough, and that our lives are not satisfying, or fulfilling. We do have only one life to live, and there is no reason to live it in vain.

Matthew had decided that he did not have enough and he was ready to believe. We, too, have to be ready to believe, because a person cannot be forced to believe. There is a famous painting at which you must look very closely, then pause and think for a minute in order to understand the artist's intent. The painting depicts Christ standing at the door of a small cottage. However, there is no knob on the door, the door has to be opened from the inside, and there is no way to get into the cottage. The truth is clear both in this painting and in life: we have to be ready to believe.

At times, that can be discouraging. A lady in one of my former congregations had been praying for thirty years that her husband would be converted. Needless to say, she had become very discouraged. Sometimes she would blame God because he didn't answer her prayers; at other times she was tempted to give up praying for her husband. Then, suddenly, one day it happened; he accepted Christ. The explanation for his decision was very simple—he had come to the time when he was ready. We can never know what makes a person ready, and we cannot predict the time or circumstance of that readiness.

When I was pastor of the First Methodist Church in Fort Worth, we kept very accurate and detailed records of people who were prospects for church membership. One Sunday I received a man, his wife, and several children into the church. After the service I discovered that we had been carrying their names in our files for seven years. According to our records, they had been called, contacted, or visited fifty-four times in seven years. No one may ever know what occurred in that family's life to make them ready, at that time, to join the church.

Nor do we really know what preceded Matthew's instant acceptance of Jesus. Maybe Matthew had become unhappy with his life. Perhaps it was when he viewed the matchless splendor of Jesus' life that he recognized the poverty and emptiness of his own heart. Doubtless he had never been exposed to the profound love, forgiveness, and mercy that he saw in Jesus. In any event, Matthew was exposed to the conditions, circumstances, or situations that made him ready to accept Jesus.

We can also guess that Matthew was willing to believe with total commitment, which is of great importance. It is one thing to need to believe, another to be ready to believe, and still something else to be ready to believe with total commitment. The evidence indicates that Matthew instantly accepted Christ with total dedication.

One of the most dramatic verses in all scripture is, "Jesus . . . saw a man called Matthew . . . and he said to him, 'Follow me.' And he rose and followed him" (Matt. 9:9). Can you imagine the scene? Matthew was sitting at his desk counting his money. Jesus came by and said, "Follow me." And, just like that, with instant acceptance, Matthew followed Jesus, willing to believe with total commitment. We have to admire Matthew's courage because immediate assent is not easy. All of us are hesitant to make a total commitment to anyone or anything without ample time to contemplate our decision.

Mark Trotter, a Methodist pastor in California, once told about a young man and woman who had been going together for a long time. Eventually, they fell deeply in love, and he decided to propose to her. He set the scene one night by driving out to a lake, and parking in the moonlight. He turned to her and said, "Darling, I want you to know that I love you more than anything else in the world. I want you to marry me. I'm not wealthy, I'm not rich. I don't have a yacht or a Rolls Royce like Johnny Green, but I do love you with all my heart."

She thought for a minute and replied, "I love you with all my heart, too, but tell me more about Johnny Green." You see, it is not easy to make that total commitment.

Our problem is that we want to become Christians by degrees. We don't want to rush into it; we don't want to be pushed into it. We don't want to be impetuous. We don't want to give everything. We want to become Christians just a little bit at a time.

Sometime ago I was staying at a motel in another city where I was preaching. My room was next to the swimming pool. Early one morning when I was working on a sermon, I glanced out my window to see a man coming to the swimming pool. He reached the edge of the pool and gingerly put his right foot into the water. He moved it around a little, and then pulled it out. Then he put his left foot in the water, but soon took it out. Next, he sat down, inched closer to the water, and slowly slid both of his feet in. Finally, he gradually lowered part of his body into the pool, still clasping the side with his hands. He raised and lowered himself once or twice, and then he went back to his room. That is exactly our approach to the Christian faith. We put one foot carefully in; we do it half-heartedly. But Matthew jumped in all the way. After he had committed himself to Jesus, he gave everything he had.

Dwight Moody was a shoe clerk before he became a famous evangelist. Recognizing his lack of training and formal education, he once said, "I am not much of a man, but Christ has all there is of me." Matthew might have said, "Jesus, I'm an extortioner, I'm a sinner, I'm a crook. I'm not much of a man, but you've got all there is of me."

Matthew's story is really our story. Is this the moment to decide that we are ready to believe?

Scripture: Matthew 9:9; Mark 2:14; 3:18; Luke 5:27-29; 6:15; Acts 1:13

Not a Word or a Deed
JAMES

CHAPTER

[9]

My wife has a small dog. Unfortunately, he's a sorry little dog, because, while he is handsome and intelligent, he is of no use whatsoever. Perhaps his uselessness began with his early success. When he was younger, he won several blue and red ribbons at dog shows. And then he decided that he was the head of our household. Now, if you want him to go outside, he prefers to stay inside. If you want him to stay inside, he insists on going out. If you ask him to come to you, he runs away. If you put a leash on him and try to walk him, he will go in the other direction. If you agreeably go that way with him, he will change directions. He is definitely not a follower; he is a leader.

There are also some people like that; some of us are just not good at following. We can lead, but we can't follow. It may be that some of us have not yet learned that often it takes more skill, more self-confidence, and more internal security to be a follower than it does to be a leader. The disciple James certainly was a follower of Jesus.

James was inaudible and invisible. Neither a word nor a deed appears in the New Testament regarding him. He probably was the son of Alphaeus, and that means he may have been the brother of Matthew. The Revised Standard Version of the Bible calls him "James the younger," which might have been a way of distinguishing this James from the other James—James the great and James the less. The Greek word used in regard to him is micros, an indication that James may have been small of stature. Since he neither speaks nor acts in the New Testament, we may look upon him as representative of the vast multitude of people who throughout their daily lives and duties contribute much good to humanity, and then pass on from this life to the next without any praise or recognition. James could well be called "the patron saint of the unrecognized."

The lesson we may learn from James is that while both the world and the church need leaders, the hope of the world as well as the hope of the church is to be found in the many people who are not leaders but who can be followers. It is only with the followers, the great masses of people who are willing to follow Christ, that the kingdom of God can come and his will be done on earth as it is in heaven. We have to have chairpersons, presidents, soloists, ministers, and all kinds of leaders in the church, but we also need many more followers. James was a follower; we ought to be followers also.

We can imagine that, in addition to being a follower, James was also an enabler because followers are always enablers. James was probably low-key and introspective. However, he enabled Peter, James, and John to be leaders. He enabled Jesus' ministry to continue and to prosper. Little is achieved without enablers.

Earl Campbell, running back of the Houston Oilers, as most of you know, is an outstanding football player. He has made many touchdowns and gained a lot of yardage. He has received most of the awards and much of the acclamation that the football world has to offer. But Earl Campbell has never forgotten who enabled him to become renowned. He has always remembered that it was the linemen who blocked the opposing players, enabling him to achieve. He has shown his gratitude to his enablers tangibly and intangibly throughout the years.

"Ensemble" is a word often used in the theatrical world. It refers to a drama, without stars, that is viewed as a whole. The program for such a production usually reads simply, "The Company," and lists all the players in alphabetical order, regardless of the importance of their roles. An ensemble production is one in which everyone has an equal part in enabling the drama to take place.

Several years ago a well-known actor achieved great success on television in our country. He was receiving a lucrative salary, his financial future was assured, and his name had almost become a household word. Then, suddenly, at what most of us would view as the peak of his career, he quit. He was quoted as saying, "I want to go to England to play with an ensemble company, so that I can learn how to be an actor. I've become a star, but I'm not an actor yet." He seems to have realized the value of being an enabler.

There are many ensemble players or enablers in every church. They are not seen, and few people know them. They never appear in the pulpit, but they are of great significance; they are the enablers. In many churches there are those who come every week to take care of the church library, do clerical tasks, help prepare for church suppers and very few people know their names.

In the church that I serve there is a small prayer group. The people pray for me and for the church every day and no one knows them. We have members of a prayer chain who pray for others. Nobody knows their names except God. I would call that "doing theology." All of these people are of the utmost importance. Very little would take place without the scores of unrecognized people who come to this church and quietly do their tasks. They enable the ministry and mission of Christ at our church.

James, too, was an ensemble player; he was an enabler. He enabled the disciples to do their work. He helped enable Jesus to do his ministry, and that is what we should do too.

James was also an accomplisher; followers are accomplishers because they are the ones who finally do the work. It is rather a strange paradox that those who just follow, who simply enable, also find that they accomplish. Those who find a job that needs doing, and then do it well, always have a sense of self-satisfaction, a sense of self-fulfillment, a sense of accomplishment. When you become a part of something that is bigger than you are, a cause that is greater than yourself, there is a thrill, there is a joy, there is a sense of accomplishment.

One day Robert Henri, the artist, was attending a showing at an art gallery in New York City. He stood before a magnificent oil painting by Sargent, admiring it. He became aware of a brawny individual standing next to him who kept murmuring to himself, "I've been given a place at last." Finally, Robert Henri turned to him, and asked, "Are you in this sort of work?" "I have been for years," the man replied, "but this is the first time I ever got on the line." Confused, Robert Henri asked, "Which is your picture?" "That one," the man answered, gesturing toward the painting in front of them. Perplexed even further, Robert Henri said, "You must be mistaken, that was painted by the great Sargent." "Yes, I think it was Sargent who painted the picture," the man replied, "but it was me who made the frame."

The frame, as we know, can make a remarkable difference in a painting. The one who makes the frame should have a sense of accomplishment; he or she deserves a feeling of self-fulfillment. And, every person who enables the gospel to happen, who enables the Good News to be spread, should have a deep sense of accomplishment.

In addition to being an accomplisher, James was also a servant and that is what we are called to be. We're called to be followers, we're called to be enablers, and we're also called to be servants. "Whosoever of you will be the chiefest," said Jesus, "shall be servant of all" (KJV). One of the finest biblical descriptions of Jesus is found in Philippians: he "made himself of no reputation, and took upon him the form of a servant" (KJV).

Servanthood, the towel and the basin, not the sword and the shield, are the symbols of Christ's disciples. James did not speak a word or do a deed that is recorded in the New Testament. He was inaudible and invisible, largely unkown to us, but he was known to God as a servant. And, that is what we are supposed to be—servants.

A colleague of mine includes a line in his Sunday bulletin that I like very much. At the end of the order of worship, there is a sentence which reads, "When the benediction has been said, the service will begin." That is correct theology. We come to church to worship, to get recreated, refueled, and recharged, only for the purpose of going out into the world to serve in the name of Christ.

On the Tomb of the Unknown Soldier in Arlington, Virginia, are inscribed these words: "Here rests in honored glory an American soldier known only to God." That could be said of many Christians. "Here is an unknown Christian who is known only to God." James is the patron saint of unrecognized servants of God. James was an unknown soldier of the cross, an unknown servant of Christ. We do not know what he said and we do not know what he did, but we do know that he was a servant of Christ.

God grant that we, too, may be numbered among the vast multitude of those who witness, work, and pray and, then, pass on without praise or recognition, thus emulating the life of the disciple James.

Scripture: Mark 15:40

The Impetuous Hero

PETER

CHAPTER

[10]

Big, bold, impulsive, adventuresome, dynamic, competent, confident, and committed; those are words that aptly describe the disciple Simon Peter. Peter was the son of Jonah, and Andrew's brother. He was first the disciple of John the Baptist, then Andrew introduced him to Christ, and he became a Christian, one of the twelve disciples.

He also became one of the three members of Christ's "executive committee"—Peter, James, and John. Among these three, his name is almost always listed first. "The Big Fisherman" was big in everything, both in his accomplishments and in his mistakes. He was always the first to speak, the first to act, and the first to react.

Jesus chose Peter to go with him up on Mount Tabor to witness the Transfiguration. Jesus also selected him to stay with him in the Garden of Gethsemane. When Jesus asked the disciples, "Who am I?" the other disciples could not answer.

It was Simon Peter who said, "Thou art the Christ, the Son of the Living God." And Jesus replied, "Blessed art thou, Simon Bar-Jona: for flesh and blood hath not revealed it unto thee, but my Father which is in heaven. . . .And upon this rock [the rock of your faith] I will build my church; and the gates of hell shall not prevail against it" (Matt. 16:17-18 KJV).

Jesus gave the keys to the kingdom to Peter. Surprisingly, it was Peter who was chosen to preach the sermon at Pentecost where three thousand persons were added to the church. After the death and resurrection of Christ, Peter became the leader of the infant church. Some scholars believe that Mark's Gospel is primarily the record of Peter's sermons. Finally, Peter found death through martyrdom, but he did not deem himself worthy to be crucified in the same way as his Lord, so legend has it that he requested to be crucified upside down.

It is true that Peter was the one who denied Christ at a critical moment, at a time of Jesus' direst need. Three times Peter denied him, saying, "I do not know the man." This was a momentary lapse of courage that reduced Peter to weeping and to shame. However, it should also be noted that at the trial of Jesus, Peter was the only disciple who had the courage to stay among the angry mob in the courtyard of the high priest. All the other disciples had already fled because they were afraid.

There are really no words to describe Simon Peter adequately. Lingual brushstrokes fail to bring to life his complexities. However, we will call him the impetuous hero because he was impulsive and tempestuous, but he was also a great hero of the faith.

We should note that Peter was always involved, never peripherally, but always totally engaged in a situation. He was usually on center stage. He appears in every scene of this scriptural drama. He was constantly speaking, acting, doing, and participating.

We have all known people like that, those who have to be in the center of everything. I remember a young college student who had to be in the thick of things. If there was a three-alarm fire, he wanted to be the first spectator; if there was an important police raid, he wanted to be first on the scene; if a drama was produced, he wanted to be the first to audition; if the President of the United States came to town, he would be first in line to greet him. There are people who want to be a part of everything.

That describes Peter. He had to participate in whatever occurred. And, to his credit, he put his energy, his enthusiasm, his talent, and his self-confidence into everything. He gave his best; he gave his all. To Peter, following Jesus meant to be completely involved and totally committed. That's what it should mean to us, too. When Jesus said, "Follow me," he meant, "Give yourself," because following Christ means giving yourself. Strangely enough, that's the way we are created; that is the way we are made. We are made for giving. If we don't give, we are trying to live against the grain of our creation.

An automobile is not made to fly, a bicycle is not made to float, and we are not made to accumulate excessively. We are made to give. A lot of people are frustrated and unhappy without knowing why. The reason is that they are victims of the psychotic disorder of plutomania—the uncontrolled drive to accumulate. That is against the grain of our creation, therefore we're miserable, frustrated, and angry. The only way we can fulfill our creative destiny is through giving. Every counselor, psychologist, and psychiatrist knows patients who could be cured if they could find the dynamic, the motivation, for giving. For in giving we find the purpose of life, the fulfillment, and the joy of life. Thus we enable God's will to be done in us and through us and on the earth as it is done in heaven.

Make no mistake about it, reluctant givers are not Christ's followers, because Christ's followers are by definition givers. And the disciple Peter gave himself.

Not only did he give himself, but he gave himself recklessly. It was Peter who ran headlong into the empty tomb. When Jesus walked on the water, the disciples and Peter watched from the boat. We can conclude that Peter wanted to be the first to greet the Master; he didn't want any of the other disciples to get ahead of him. We might imagine Peter impatiently crying out, "Master, can I come to you?" I have an idea that Jesus' answer was tongue-in-cheek, "Yes, Peter come on," so Peter started walking across the water. The winds were heavy. He was suddenly afraid and he sank; he went down crying, "Lord, save me." Reckless, impetuous? Yes, he was. Yet we admire his instinctive spontaneity. God's gift of his own Son to die upon a cross was a reckless gift, was it not? But no less a gift than that could wash our sins away.

Peter gave injudiciously in imitation of God's own reckless gift. And God expects us to give like that. Every child has learned the Bible verse, "God loves a cheerful giver." Cheerful is translated from the Greek word *hilaros* (hilarious). We ought to be hilarious givers.

I was a child of the depression. The first schoolboy allowance I had was ten cents a week. Even during the depression you couldn't get into a lot of trouble on ten cents. A favorite phrase at our house was, "Be sure you bring back the change." If I was given some money to go to the grocery store to buy a loaf of bread, I heard, "Be sure you bring the change back!" When I returned, the money was counted out because, in those days, every single penny was important. When I was twelve years old, my father gave me five dollars one day to go to the state fair. I was expecting the usual reminder, "Bring back the change." Instead he said, "Spend it all. Have fun!" That was some experience! I wasn't expected to bring back any change and I didn't. I spent it all hilariously, rashly, for whatever I wanted. It is fun when you can spend heedlessly.

The Bible says that we are supposed to tithe, to give one-tenth of what we receive. Some people give 10 percent legalistically, but the tithe is not intended to be a law. It is supposed to be a joyous, happy, hilarious experience of giving.

A man I know keeps a separate bank account and calls it his tithing account. The checks for this account bear his name and the words, "Tithing Account." He is a salesman and every time he receives a commission he deposits one-tenth of it in this account. He receives a genuine thrill, a tremendous amount of exitement to be able to give recklessly from that account. He has told me that sometimes he does not have the money to take a vacation or do some of the other things he wants to do, but he always has money to give. I've heard him say over and over again what joy he experiences in giving that money away.

Not only should we give our money hilariously, but, like Peter, we should also give our time, our talents, our skills, our resources, our energy, and our enthusiasm. We ought to give all of these away joyously. These gifts of ourselves make possible Christ's ministry through the church. They make the world a better place in which to live. And, they enable us to make some compensating contribution for the privilege of living on this earth. Peter gave, he gave recklessly, and so should we.

As we have seen, Peter also made mistakes; but God forgave his mistakes and blessed his giving. Try to imagine, if you can, how Jesus must have felt toward Peter. Surely there must have been times when Jesus was irritated with him. There must have also been instances when he was angry or impatient with him. But Jesus knew that he was invaluable as a disciple. Now, try to go from the sublime to the ridiculous—perhaps Jesus felt about Peter a little bit like a football coach feels about his quarterback who fumbles five times in the game, but completes eighteen passes and runs for more than a hundred yards. In spite of the fumbles, a coach can't do without a quarterback like that. And, in spite of Peter's impetuous, impulsive, tempestuous nature, Jesus must have thought he was very valuable and so he forgave his mistakes and blessed his giving.

Peter may very well have been aware of that. If Mark's Gospel is indeed a record of Peter's sermons, that means Peter himself told about his denial of Jesus. Peter could say "When he needed me most, I failed him. I denied him three times. What shame! How I cried, but he forgave me. Miracle of miracles, he forgave me." That is proof positive that he will forgive us of our sins. He forgave Peter his mistakes, and he blessed his giving.

Peter preached the sermon at Pentecost. Jesus blessed Peter because Peter helped make possible Christ's teaching and ministry. Peter provided for the continuity of the Christian faith after the death and resurrection of Christ by being a strong, aggressive leader of the infant church. His giving made possible the fulfillment of his own life and the lives of others. His influence has passed on down through the centuries to us. God also forgives our mistakes and blesses our giving. When we give recklessly and hilariously we're going to make some mistakes, but God forgives and blesses us. The Bible says, "Bring all your tithes into the storehouse of God and see if I won't pour out more blessings than you're able to absorb" (paraphrase). When we give, God blesses every giver.

Regrettably, some people have never learned to

give. They would like to give, but they just don't know how. People have told me they would like to give, but, for some reason, they cannot bring themselves to actually do so. But those who have learned how to give, and those who have learned how to give hilariously, will inevitably testify to great blessings. For giving is not only a requirement of discipleship, it is the secret of life itself. The only way to get life is to give life. Jesus made that very clear. He said in effect, "If you try to keep your life you will lose it, but if you will lose your life, if you will give your life away, then you will find it." Francis Bacon expressed the same idea thus:

> What I kept I lost,
> What I saved is gone,
> What I gave away I still have.

Every hilarious giver knows the truth of those words.

You see, we should realize that what we have given away is all we are going to take into the life beyond. We can't take anything else. We can't take our cars or our houses or even our pocket change. But, we are going to take everything we have given away. And, when we stand before the judgment seat of God that is all we will have to show him; nothing else except what we gave away.

Many of my childhood years were spent near the

Mississippi River, first in Memphis, Tennessee, and then in Paducah, Kentucky. I have a lot of happy memories about "Ol' Man River." The Mississippi River flows into the Gulf of Mexico where it empties itself totally, completely into the Gulf; it withholds nothing. The sun draws the water out of the Gulf. Then the winds blow the clouds back up to the head of the Mississippi where they pour their water back into the river, so that the Mississippi River always gets back everything it gives.

Do you want life today? Are you looking for real life, fulfilled life, satisfying life, joyous life? If so, try giving your life away. If you give it away then you will receive it back again and again, forgiven and blessed.

Scripture: Mark 14:66-72

A Daring Choice
SIMON

CHAPTER

[11]

Perhaps of all the disciples Jesus chose, Simon the Zealot was the most daring choice. It was a bold choice because Simon belonged to a revolutionary group of hotheaded patriots called the Zealots who were sworn to resist the rule of Rome and to overthrow the Roman conquerers by any means, fair or foul.

Matthew, the tax gatherer who sold out to the Romans, said, in effect, "There's nothing we can do about the Romans, so we might as well cooperate with them." But Simon not only refused to sell out, he also refused to make peace with the Romans. He was dedicated to their defeat by war, by violence, by any method possible. Matthew and Simon might have disliked each other intensely prior to the time they became disciples, because they were seeking diametrically opposite goals. Simon wanted to fight the Romans; Matthew wanted to join them.

Jesus' choice of Simon was also a daring one because evidently Simon was only interested in the earthly kingdom, and Jesus was interested in the heavenly kingdom. Simon was willing to shed blood for his cause, and Jesus was opposed to all force and violence. Jesus must have decided that if he could turn the passionate, zealousness of Simon toward the goals of God's will, then Simon could become a power for righteousness. That is exactly what happened.

It is important for us to remember that Simon the Zealot before Christ was also Simon the Zealot after he became a disciple of Christ. He is mentiond once in each of the three Synoptic Gospels, and once in the Acts of the Apostles. After he became a Christian he was still known as Simon the Zealot.

We can gather that it was important to Jesus to have at least one of the disciples who was extraordinarily ardent in his commitment to the fulfillment of his ministry. Simon the Zealot was vigorously enthusiastic about the mission of Christ.

The word enthusiasm comes from the Greek words *en theos* meaning "God in you," or, "full of God." That is who Simon was, and that is who we ought to be. To be sure, one test of our Christianity is whether or not we are enthusiastic, whether God is in us, whether we are full of God.

Enthusiasm is one criterion of the Christian because enthusiasm is partial evidence of our love. If you love someone you are enthusiastic about it; it is impossible for you to be apathetic, calm, or unmoved.

One of my favorite stories is about the old man who had reached the venerable age of one hundred one. He and his wife, who was ninety-seven, had been married for seventy-five years. One cold, snowy day they were sitting in the living room in their rocking chairs before a roaring fire. The old man was rather deaf. His wife kept looking at him, her eyes filled with admiration. Finally, she said, "Zeb, I want you to know I'm proud of you." He said, "I'm tired of you too, Mandy."

We have to be enthusiastic about love. If we truly love God, we will be enthusiastic about that love. Jesus said that the first commandment is, "Thou shalt love the Lord thy God with all thy heart and with all thy soul, and with all thy mind" (Matt. 22:37 KJV). He might have said, "You must love with enthusiasm."

Many of you remember the woman, perhaps it was Mary, who came to Jesus one day and poured a bottle of expensive perfume on his head, as a symbol of her love and dedication. The disciples were very angry. They grabbed her protesting, "You shouldn't do that! You could have sold the perfume for enough money to feed a lot of the poor people around here" (paraphrase). Jesus stopped them and said, in effect, "No, no. What she has done is wonderful. It's great. For what she has done she will always be remembered, because she gave what she has. Her love for me has been made evident by her enthusiastic gift." *En theos;* she was full of God.

True love, as many of us know, is always enthusiastically extravagant. It can never give enough. Even after it has given all, it still thinks the gift is too small. If you love God, you will give evidence of it through your enthusiastic words, deeds, and gifts.

I recently received a letter from a lady in our congregation; she also enclosed her pledge card. "I am retired now," she wrote. "I only have a small pension." She mentioned the amount of her pension, and then she wrote, "My pledge is one-tenth of that pension." Her last sentence read, "Oh, how I wish I could do more!" Her enthusiasm was confirmation of her love for God, her love for Christ, and her love for the church.

Simon loved Christ, and he loved the causes for which Christ gave himself. The evidence of Simon's love is to be found in his zealousness, his enthusiasm.

Enthusiasm is also the evidence of our convictions. If we really believe something, we will be enthusiastic about it. At times, it is difficult to tell whether some people actually believe something or not, because they are casual, uncertain, unconvinced, and unexcited. A professor I once had in seminary never really convinced his students that he believed what he taught. He was offhand, indifferent, and almost nonchalant about his subject. If we really believe something, we will be ebullient about it.

A critic once wrote to a London newspaper regarding Clement Attlee, saying of Mr. Attlee, "He brings to the fierce struggle the tepid enthusiasm of a lazy summer afternoon at a cricket match." I've known people who were just about that enthusiastic regarding their convictions about God. The writer of the Letter of James talks about having the form of religion but lacking the power. We, too, know many people who have the form of religion. They pray every day; they read the Bible; they go to church and participate in worship by knowing the proper time to sit, stand, and kneel. However, they are uninspired in their convictions. They have the form of religion, but they lack the power of religion. That is also one of the sins of the church. Some people don't go to church just because they are bored by it. The church has convictions, but it sometimes lacks enthusiasm.

While on vacation recently I attended a church, a beautiful church with an impressive sanctuary. It was a lovely service of worship, including all the proper prayers and responses. It was faithful to the liturgical requirements of appropriate worship in its proper theological framework. The minister read a very fine sermon in a quiet monotone. As I walked out of the church after the service, I said to myself, "So what?" It seemed to me that most of us in the service had no objection to anything that was said or done, we were just bored. That is an example of having the form of religion, but not the power of it.

Bishop Gerald Kennedy said the gospel ought to be like a newsboy standing on a street corner shouting, "Extra, extra. Read all about it. Good news! Good news!" No one can be convinced unless we convince them, and we cannot convince them unless we are *en theos,* full of God, enthusiastic about our convictions. In Shakespeare's *Henry VIII,* Cardinal Wolsey speaks one of the most famous exit lines when he says, "Had I but served God with the same zeal I served my king, He would not in mine age have left me naked to my enemies." Indeed, we often serve our employer or something else with more zeal than we serve God.

Several years ago I went to a Dallas Cowboys football game. I had one of the less expensive tickets and was so far away from the field that I could hardly see the game. Therefore, I became interested in a man seated four or five rows below me. He was extemely excited about the game. He jumped up, yelled, threw his hat, and screamed. Since I couldn't see the game, I started watching the man instead. It was fascinating because he was so enthusiastic. He was utterly convinced that the Cowboys had the best team, that they were going to win. Then, suddenly, as he turned to lead all of us in a cheer I saw his face for the first time—he was a member of my church. I had never seen him that excited about God. He was totally persuasive in his beliefs about the Dallas Cowboys, but he wouldn't have persuaded anyone by the evidence of his beliefs about God. How sad, for our enthusiasm is the verification of our convictions. Simon the Zealot's fervency and enthusiasm substantiated his strong convictions.

In addition to being the evidence of our convictions, enthusiasm is also proof of our commitment. True commitment to anything reveals itself in our enthusiasm. If you are apathetic, unenthusiastic about your job, you probably have very little commitment to it and are being unfair both to yourself and to your employer. But, if you are enthusiastic about your work, if you can't wait to get up in the morning to go to the office, then it is obvious that you have a commitment to your job.

All sports fans know who Vince Lombardi was. He took over the Green Bay Packers football team when it was dispirited, defeated, and demoralized. They had lost almost every game. Vince Lombardi called the team together and said, "Gentlemen, we're going to have a great football team. We're going to win games. We're going to learn to block; we're going to learn to tackle. We're going to learn to run. We're going to outplay our opposition. We're going to win! And how is this to be done? You're to have confidence in me and enthusiasm for my system of play. And, hereafter I want you to think of only three things: your family, your religion, and the Green Bay Packers, in that order. Let enthusiasm take hold of you right now!"

Most football enthusiasts know what happened. That team, those same players started winning games. The Green Bay Packers became the envy of the football world. Vince Lombardi developed what is probably the greatest football dynasty in professional football history. When the Green Bay Packers took the field, no one had to ask any questions about their commitment. Their enthusiasm was obvious. They were eager to get on the field; they couldn't wait to get in the game. Their enthusiasm gave evidence of their total commitment.

It is the same in our religious faith. If we are not enthusiastic, if we are lukewarm, if we have no fervor, no zeal, we can be sure that we have no commitment. Simon was *en theos,* full of

God, enthusiastic. That was the evidence of his commitment.

A lady in my church writes me letters rather often. They are wonderful letters. I enjoy them, and I look forward to reading them. She first started worshiping with us by television. She did this for over a year, and then one Sunday she decided she would come to church. When she did, she was surprised. In fact, she was overcome by the unexpected warmth, the friendliness, and the caring concern of our congregation. And so she kept coming, Sunday after Sunday, until one Sunday she joined the church. She remembers the month and the date that she first visited church. She can recall every detail of that day. She also remembers the date of the Sunday she became a member. She remembers the title of the anthems the choir sang that day, and she remembers the sermon theme. She even remembers the title of the hymn that was sung as she walked down the aisle. She always closes her letters with a word of thanksgiving and gratitude for the saving grace of God and Jesus Christ, and for the church which served as God's instrument to bring her into that saving fellowship.

Is there any doubt about her commitment? Not at all. Her enthusiasm gives ample evidence of the profound depth of her commitment to Christ and to the church.

Some of us need this more than anything else. More than anything else we need to be *en theos*, full of God, zealous and enthusiastic like Simon. We need that in our love, in our convictions, and in our commitment.

Scripture: Matthew 10:4; Mark 3:18; Luke 6:15; Acts 1:13

Betrayer or Betrayed?

JUDAS

CHAPTER

[12]

Judas Iscariot, probably named after Judas Maccabaeus, not only possessed a marvelous namesake, but he also apparently came from a fine home. We do not know his mother's name; his father's name was Simon. His parents were devoted Jews. They customarily attended the synagogue and reared Judas Iscariot to attend regularly and observe the law.

Judas' position in the apostolic band was that of treasurer. Evidently he exhibited an expertise in financial matters, and so the disciples entrusted him with their funds. The Gospels do not indicate any criticism of the way he handled that responsibility. His deed of treachery came when, for thirty shekels of silver, he betrayed Jesus with a kiss.

A consideration of the result of his act is important as we try to draw a picture of Judas. He was immediately unhappy with what he had done. It was clear to him that his scheme had not worked out as he had hoped. He said, "I have betrayed innocent blood." He returned the thirty shekels and then committed suicide by hanging. For his deed of betrayal, he became the symbol of disloyalty for all succeeding generations.

There are many possible interpretations of Judas' act. Scholars do not agree at this point. A possible interpretation is that Judas was not the betrayer, but the betrayed. I want to suggest to you that Judas Iscariot did not intend that Jesus should die, that he did not understand the result of his action in turning Christ over to his enemies, that in the mind of Judas, at least, his action would result in Jesus being a hero at best, a martyr at worst. It seems possible to me that Judas was not the betrayer, but the betrayed.

Isn't it reasonable to assume that Judas may have been betrayed by his lack of patience? He was a "now" person. Judas wanted things to happen immediately; he didn't like to wait. He had been with Jesus for three years; he had been committed, loyal, and loving. He had done what he was supposed to do. But now he was tired of waiting. Jesus was to bring in the kingdom, and it hadn't come. Judas decided that he had waited as long as he could, as long as he would, and so he decided to act.

This is the scenario he may have written in his mind: he would betray Jesus into the hands of his enemies and that betrayal would force Jesus to act. It would compel Jesus to call upon his supernatural powers, to produce a miracle, to say the magic word that would establish the kingdom of Israel. After all, had not Judas seen Jesus bring back to life persons who had been dead? Wasn't he the Son of God? Couldn't he do anything he wanted to do? Couldn't he perform that miracle if he wished? Surely he would not allow himself to be crucified on a cross by his enemies when he had the power to avoid it, when he could perform a miracle that would get rid of the Romans, establish the kingdom of Israel, and save himself from death. If that had happened, Judas would have been a hero. Judas' logic seems perfectly sound.

If we follow this line of reasoning, Judas' suicide can be explained. He did away with himself because his plan didn't work. In truth, it was a monumental failure.

In plotting his strategy, Judas did not realize that Jesus could not be compelled to act in a way that was unworthy of his divine call. So, instead of the desired results, Judas caused Christ to be turned into the hands of his enemies who would crucify him on a cross. Judas was devastated by the failure of his plan. He returned the money, admitted his terrible deed, and committed suicide by hanging. Judas may have been betrayed by his lack of patience.

He may also have been betrayed by his lack of insight and understanding. One of Judas' problems was that he was a single-issue disciple. The only thing he was really interested in was ridding the country of the Romans and establishing Israel as God's kingdom. He thought Jesus had come to lead that revolution. That's all he was really concerned about.

Judas did not comprehend the balanced view of Jesus' ministry. He did not understand the total agenda of Jesus' mission. He did not have the insight to see that Christ had come to do more than just get rid of the Romans, to do more than just save Israel. He could not see that Jesus had come to save the last and the least of the lost, even the Romans; to pronounce the Word of God that all people are his children and that all can be the recipients of his grace, love and forgiveness. Judas just did not understand that God does not force or compel, that God is not a divine puppeteer who manipulates the world to suit his own desired ends. He did not have the insight to see that God would not force a miracle. Judas was betrayed by his shortsightedness, by the paucity of his understanding.

In addition, he was betrayed by his lack of trust. Judas was driven by the rightness of his cause, motivated to make it happen. And, finally, he felt lonely, in agony and anguish, because it had not happened. It did not appear that it would occur any time soon, and, finally, he no longer trusted Christ to do it. He no longer believed that God could bring it off, so he took matters into his own hands.

Perhaps, of all the disciples, Judas is the greatest example for us. What can we learn from him? He teaches us that we are so like him. Our motives are honest; our intentions are good. Yet, we too manage somehow to betray Christ, to get rid of him, to hand him over to his enemies. In that respect, we are like Judas.

We, also, betray Christ by our impatience. The psalmist cried, "How long, O Lord, how long?" and so do we. At times, I feel depressed, I feel a sense of despair, and I have cried, "How long, O Lord, will you let this go on? We have been promised life and we have received death. We have been promised love and there is hatred. God, you spoke to us about peace, but there is only war. You said I could have my life fulfilled, instead it is only frustrated. You told me about joy, but I only have sorrow. Dear God, you spoke of the kingdom of God in society, but instead there are thieves, rapists, drug peddlers, and immorality of every kind. You said that your will would be done on earth; instead there is the threat of total destruction. You talked about feeding the hungry and clothing the naked, but instead there is rising unemployment and more people are hungry and more people are naked. How long, O Lord, shall we be patient with you?"

Others ask, "God, why must my loved one die?" Or, in some instances, "Why, why, why do you not let her die?" The questions are unceasing, "Why must I continue to suffer? Why did you let my child become addicted to drugs? Why is my loved one an alcoholic?"

We wonder how long we can be patient with God. Yet, when we do so, we forget that God is the God of patience, that one day is a thousand or maybe a million years in his sight; that the judgment of history is not delivered today, that the justice of life is not evident now, that the final examination has not yet been taken and the ultimate answer has not been offered. We are so restive that we give up on God and when we do, we betray him because we are impatient.

We also betray him by our lack of insight and understanding. Again, we are like Judas. We are often single-issue Christians. We lack the balanced view of the totality of God's will and Christ's ministry. That is one of the troubles with the world, one of the troubles with society, and one of the troubles with our country.

Several weeks ago I had the privilege of visiting with a United States senator. I do not always agree with him, but I respect him tremendously. I raised the question of single-issue people in the political world. His response was, "The people back home have no idea of the incredible pressure that is put upon us by single-issue people—lobbyists, pressure groups, who just have one issue to win, one issue to press." He might also admit the single-issue pressure of the party. We hear, "Vote the straight party line," regardless of your personal conscience or convictions. There are those who have been punished when they did not do so. The question of single-issue politicians reminds me of what Will Rogers said, "We don't need any more Democratic senators. We don't need any more Republican senators. What we need is some United States senators."

That is also true of Christians. We can't be judgmental because we are often single-issue Christians. For instance, I have to be very careful that the church does not become a single issue for me, that I don't find myself trapped into the temptation of believing that the kingdom of God resides at our church, and that what we do is the only thing that is important in our city or in the world. We are an important part of the city, but we are not all of it by any means. It is necessary that I force myself out into the world to align myself with other eleemosynary causes and institutions. I must be sure that our church does not become a single issue either.

This is true of all good things. There are those who are only concerned about a cure for cancer, or diabetes research, or heart disease. There are others who are only interested in minorities, or majorities, or the poor, or the rich, or child abuse. Some people are only interested in improving our penal institutions. By observing these people, we might think that there is no other problem in the world except the one that consumes their interest.

We are guilty of this narrowness in our faith. We find one element and focus on it to the exclusion of all others. There are people who center on prayer. For them prayer is the single issue. That's all they talk about, all they read about. Or, there are people who want to focus on the issue of individual salvation. That's their answer, their single issue. There are others who center on social salvation as opposed to individual salvation. We can even do this with the Bible. There are those for whom the Bible is the single issue of the Christian faith. They study the Bible, memorize the Bible; that is all there is for them. In technical terms that is called "bibliolatry," the idolatry of the Bible.

Single-issue people may listen to a minister preach a sermon, but may actually hear only one sentence of it. They can assume that one sentence represents the alpha and omega of that church's beliefs, and they may disagree with it. And then they say, "Aha! I thought that's what they were like. I'll never go back to that church again!" Or, someone may read something they disagree with in a church paper and vow never to have anything to do with the Christian faith again. When we lose sight of the total picture, the entirety of the gospel, the whole will of God, in favor of only a part, then we betray Christ and our Christian faith.

And, like Judas, we betray God by our lack of trust. We begin to think that we can handle life all by ourselves. Or, we think we can do it better than God, and so we take matters into our own hands. We begin to solve our own problems, find our own happiness, set our own priorities. We still believe in God, but we are fearful that he cannot handle the situation without our help.

We make jokes about doing that. People say to me, "I trust God for this, but I'm going to help him out." They smile as if they are being facetious, but they are very serious about it. They have no intention of turning that problem over to God. They believe that God must have their assistance, and that, in fact, they are more necessary to the situation than God is. So, we become self-appointed general managers of the universe, and self-appointed general managers of our lives, of our own destinies, and sometimes self-appointed general managers of someone else's destiny because we really do not trust God.

I remember a lady coming to me with a very serious problem. She told me about it, and I asked, "What have you done?" She related all she had done, and when she had finished, I said, "I can't think of anything else you can do. You've covered everything I would have suggested. I cannot imagine one other single thing that you could do that would help the situation, so having done all you can do, turn loose of the problem. Let go of it. Trust God." She said, "You mean completely?" "I mean completely," I assured her. "Let it go; turn it over to God, trust him." "Oh", she protested, "I could never do that." When we fail to trust God, then we betray him and ourselves.

Now, let us shift the scene to the Upper Room. There Jesus and the disciples met for the Passover Feast, the Last Supper, the serving of the Holy Communion, and the washing of the feet of the disciples. Just imagine the picture. Finally, Jesus says, "One of you will betray me." The Gospels say that each of the disciples in turn asks the question, "Is it I, Lord?" In Matthew's Gospel, Judas asks, "Is it I, Master?"

The answer is, "No, Judas, it's not you. It's me. It's us."

Scripture: Matthew 26:14-16, 47-50; 27:3-10